Elementary   **Student Book**

ENGLISH ZONE

Denny Newburn and Gary Underwood

Longman — an imprint of Pearson Education

www.pearsoned.co.nz

Your comments on this book are welcome at
feedback@pearsoned.co.nz

Pearson Education New Zealand Limited

46 Hillside Road
Glenfield
Auckland 10
New Zealand

All rights reserved; no part of this publication may be reproduced; stored in a retrieval system, or transmitted in any form or by any means, electronic, mechanical, photocopying, recording or otherwise, without prior written permission of the publishers.

© Pearson Education New Zealand Limited 2003

First published 2003

Produced by Underwood Consulting and Publishing

Underwood
Consulting and Publishing

Designed by Brendan Halyday Design
Illustrations and Cover design by Craig Longmuir
Edited by Valerie Sayce
Printed In Malaysia, KVP

ISBN 0 582 54699 0

Authors' acknowledgements

The authors and the publisher would like to thank the following people for permission to reproduce material in this book:

Sail New Zealand, Viking Cruises Ltd, Auckland; Dolphin Discoveries <www.dolphinz.co.nz>; Universal Mail New Zealand; Interisland Line, division of Tranz Rail Ltd; Sutcliffe Laboratories Pty Ltd; Novartis Consumer Health Australasia Pty Ltd Auckland; Sanitarium Health Food Company; Band-Aid ® registered trademark of Johnson & Johnson; Blockbuster Video; Heinz Watties; Norman Bilborough 'Jonah Lomu', from School Journal Pt 3 no. 2 1999; Ken Nesbitt, 'Back from Mars'; Linda Knaus and Ken Nesbitt, 'Willie's Wart'; Rotorua Daily Post, 'Discovering the world of pies' and 'Smallest boat, shortest trip, biggest fish' by Cherie Taylor; Zambesi; NZGirl Ltd <www.nzgirl.co.nz>; Cathy Campbell from NZ Fashion Week.

All other photos in this book are copyright of Gary Underwood. Every effort has been made to trace the holders of copyrighted articles, extracts and photography, but if any omission can be rectified the publishers will be pleased to make the necessary arrangements.

Contents

Unit		Page
1.	Getting To Know You	4
2.	I Need Help to …	14
3.	I'm Feeling Good … I Think?	24
4.	Exploring New Zealand	34
5.	Healthy Food or Fast Food?	44
	How Much Do You Remember? Units 1–5	54
6.	Good, Better, Best	58
7.	The Fashion of Looking Good	68
8.	Working for a Living	78
9.	Please, Can I Drive the Car?	88
10.	Yesterday and Today	98
	How Much Do You Remember? Units 6–10	108

Unit 1 — Getting to Know You

Grammar: Present simple tense: uses, form, negatives, questions. Apostrophes as possessives and contractions. Introductions: *my name is, his name is, he's from.*

Vocabulary: Relationship words: *mother, father.* Nationalities: *Japanese, Korean.* Numbers in relation to age and time.

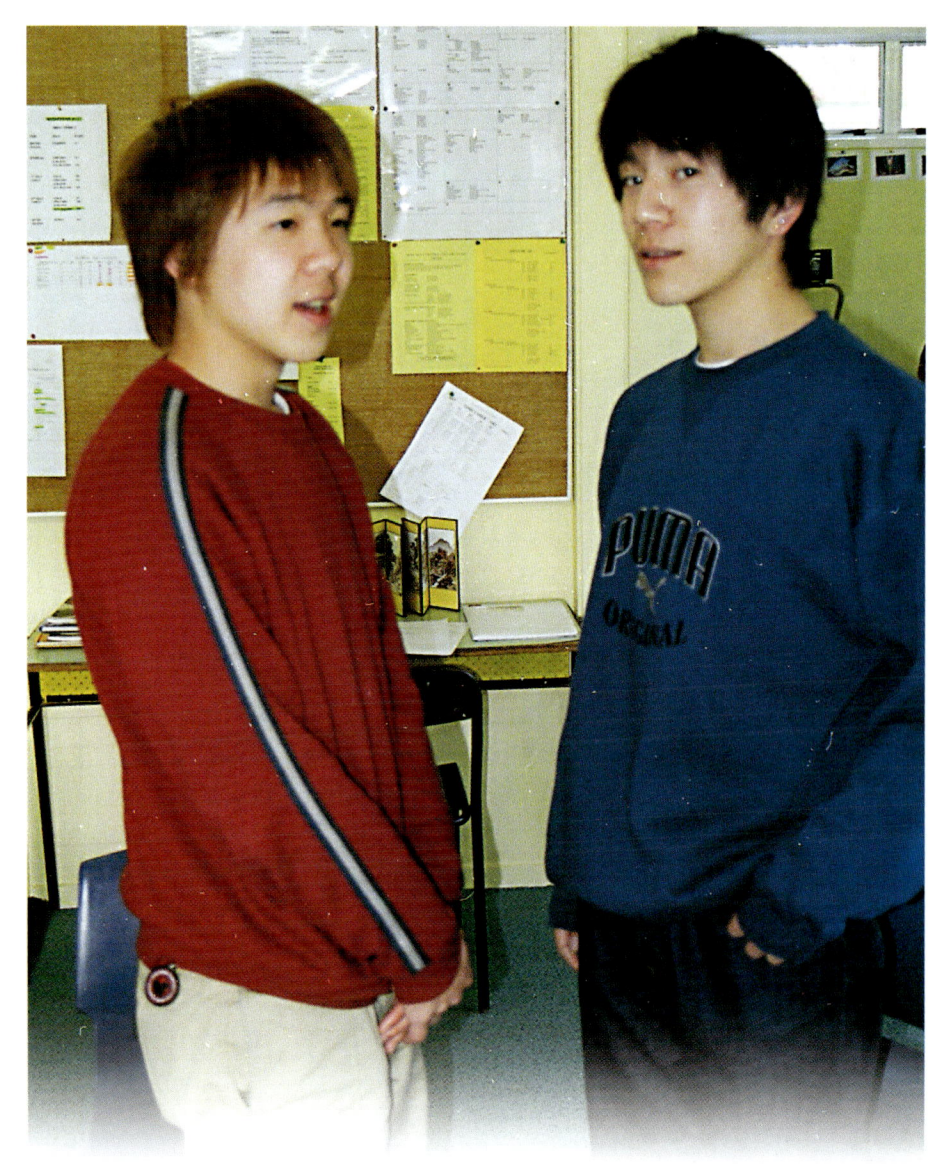

2. **Taking it in turn, write your first name on the board.**

   One class member will then attempt to line up all the students in alphabetical order. Try to decide for yourself who will be next to go in line, before the student is asked.

3. **Find a different partner, and ask each other the following questions.**

   a. What's your name?
   b. How old are you?
   c. Where are you from?
   d. How long have you been in New Zealand?
   e. Do you play sport?
   f. What do you do in your spare time?

4. **Match the title with the category of person by drawing a line between the title and the correct description.**

Mr	unmarried woman
Mrs	man – married or single
Ms	woman – married or single
Miss	married woman

STARTER

1. **Choose one person in the room you do not know and introduce yourself.**

Use the name you want the teacher to call you. This may be your new NZ name. Find out their name, where they are from and then introduce them to someone else.

Example: Hello, my name is Yuichi. What's your name? I'm from China. Where are you from?

Brendan, this is Keiko. He's from Japan.

4

5. List in alphabetical order all the objects you can see in the classroom.

_____

_____

_____

_____

_____

_____

_____

6. Write the correct form of the verb in brackets in the following sentences.

Example: *My friend goes (go) to school in Auckland.*

a. I _____ (*go*) to school in Wellington.

b. The teacher _____ (*come*) to school by car.

c. I _____ (*come*) to school by bike.

d. They all _____ (*eat*) their lunch outside.

e. We _____ (*eat*) our lunch in the hall.

f. He _____ (*eat*) his lunch with us.

g. I _____ (*be*) 15 years old.

h. My friend _____ (*be*) 16 years old.

7. Look at the family tree and answer the questions below.

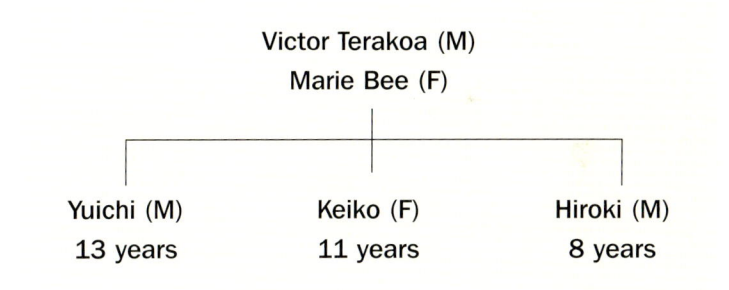

Victor Terakoa (M)
Marie Bee (F)

Yuichi (M)   Keiko (F)   Hiroki (M)
13 years   11 years   8 years

a. Who is Victor's wife? _____

b. Who is Hiroki's sister? _____

c. Who are Keiko's brothers? _____

d. How old is Yuichi? _____

e. Who is Marie's husband? _____

English Zone Elementary Student Book

8. Read through the Grammar section about the use of verbs in formal and informal language.

a. Listen to Tapescript 1 and complete the paragraph below.

My name is Keiko. I _____ 11 years old. I have _____ brothers and no sisters. We live with our _____ . Their Kiwi names are Victor and Marie.

b. Rewrite the sentences using the contracted form of the verbs.

_____

_____

_____

_____

9. Listen to Tapescript 2 and write down the numbers you hear.

a. _____ b. _____ c. _____ d. _____

e. _____ f. _____ g. _____ h. _____

i. _____ j. _____

11. Complete the following questions about William.

a. What is William doing in New Zealand?

_____

b. Where is he from? _____

c. How old is he? _____

12. Complete the following questions about Mariko.

a. Where is Mariko from? _____

b. What does she do? _____

c. What's her phone number? _____

13. Complete the following questions about Bayu.

a. How old is Bayu? _____

b. Who is he living with in New Zealand? _____

c. What country does he come from? _____

14. Using a large photograph of yourself create your own large ID card.

When you have added your personal details, but not your phone number, place it with all the other student ID cards on the wall to create a large display of everyone in the class.

LISTENING

10. Listen to Tapescript 3 and write down the details about each speaker on the ID cards.

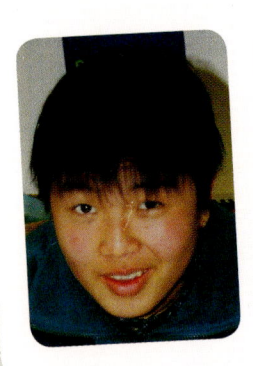

Person A ID Card
Name: _____
Age: _____
Nationality: _____
Occupation: _____
Phone No: _____

Person B ID Card
Name: _____
Age: _____
Nationality: _____
Occupation: _____
Phone No: _____

Person C ID Card
Name: _____
Age: _____
Nationality: _____
Occupation: _____
Phone No: _____

Jonah

by Norman Bilbrough

Jonah Lomu

' … Jonah's sporting career began early. At twenty-one he was the superstar of world rugby. But it wasn't always easy for him. Jonah was born in Auckland on 12 May 1975. His parents are Tongan and he was sent back to Tonga to learn his family's culture. Five years later, he returned to South Auckland …

When Jonah was nineteen, he was selected to play for the All Blacks against France. He played two games on the wing – and he has especially bad memories of the second game in Auckland, when he missed vital tackles. It was a hard introduction to top rugby for Jonah, and he nearly turned to league. But then came the 1995 World Cup, and he was selected for the black jersey again.

" I was hungry," he says. "All I wanted to do was pull on the black jersey, show everyone I could score tries … show everyone I could defend."

And he did. The high point for him was the semi-final against England. He scored four tries that day. But after each game, Jonah was exhausted. In 1996, he played against the Barbarians in England, and after the match, he had to lie in bed for three days, barely able to move. Not long after that, he was told that he had a serious kidney disease.

Fortunately, with the help of doctors and with nine months off rugby, Jonah was well enough to play in the 1998 Super 12 series.'

(From Jonah Lomu, by Norman Bilbrough. School Journal Pt 3 no.2 1999.)

READING

What do you know?

What is New Zealand's most popular national winter sport for males?

Can you name two or three famous NZ rugby players?

What do the All Blacks wear when they are playing rugby?

15. Read the article on Jonah Lomu to answer the following questions.

a. What nationality is Jonah Lomu?

b. When was Jonah born?

c. Where was he born?

d. How old was he when he was selected for the All Blacks?

e. What position did he play in against France?

f. What was the high point for Jonah Lomu?

g. What problems did he have in 1996?

h. Who helped him recover?

i. How long did he have off rugby?

j. What was the series he played in 1998?

WRITING/SPEAKING

Who What Where When Why

"Why did you come to NZ?"

"I came to learn English."

16. Write five questions you could ask another student in the class about themselves.

Leave a space under each question so that you can write down the answer. Ask your teacher to check your questions before you use them.

17. Ask another student your questions and record the answers.

Year 10 — Class Questionnaire

Question	Student 1	Student 2
1. Why did you come to New Zealand?	To learn English	
2. When did you arrive?	2 months ago	
3. How long have you been studying English?		

18. Using the answers you have been given, write a short biography of the person you interviewed. Do NOT mention their name.

Example: _____ *was born in Thailand in 1986 and has lived in New Zealand for 6 months. He likes to play golf and he likes learning English in New Zealand. He is living with a homestay family, and he hopes to go to university in New Zealand.*

19. When you have finished writing the biography, pin it up on the wall and the teacher will give it a number.

Each student must then read each of the biographies and write down the number, and whose biography they think it is. After everyone has done this, your teacher will to see who has correctly matched the biographies.

20. After reading all the biographies collect a form from your teacher.

Fill in as many details as you can about five people you have read about. After completing the form, write sentences about what you have learned.

Example: *Three people in my class come from China. Two people want to go to university in New Zealand.*

Student survey results

	Person 1	Person 2	Person 3	Person 4	Person 5
Home country					
Reasons for coming to NZ					
Length of time in NZ					
Accommodation (homestay/hostel/flat/family)					
Leisure activities					
Hopes for the future					

English Zone Elementary Student Book

Curriculum Vitae

Names: **Hahona** (Surname)   **Ryo** (First name)

Address: **1 Main st, Auckland**

Phone number: _____   Mobile: **021 356 1175**

DOB: **1985**

Nationality: **Japanese**

Occupation: **student**

Marital status: _____

Hobbies/interests: **computers and guitar**

Sports: **Rugby union**

Curriculum Vitae

Names: **Wei Lei** (Surname)   **Xiao** (First name)

Address: **36 Hopoate st, Wellington**

Phone number: **33 2234**   Mobile: _____

DOB: **1987**

Nationality: **chinese**

Occupation: **student**

Marital status: _____

Hobbies/interests: **computer games**

Sports: **Basketball**

Curriculum Vitae

Names: **Hyn** (Surname)   **Su** (First name)

Address: **377 Jones ave, Rotorua**

Phone number: _____   Mobile: **027 496 204**

DOB: **1986**

Nationality: **korean**

Occupation: **student**

Marital status: _____

Hobbies/interests: **Internet and computers**

Sports: **soccer**

APPLICATION

Discuss the meaning of CV (Curriculum Vitae) with your teacher. What is a CV? Why does everyone need one? What information should you be collecting now to put into your CV?

21. Collect the following information to use in your CV.

a. Your personal details: name, age, nationality, occupation, address, phone number.
b. Details of your education so far. Include the schools you have attended, number of years of education and qualifications achieved.
c. The sports you play.
d. What you like to do in your spare time.
e. Four or five sentences about yourself, describing your personality.

22. Ask your teacher to check what you have written to ensure there are no mistakes and that all the information you will need has been written down.

23. Collect a CV form from your teacher. Use the headings on the form to compose the first one to two pages of your CV.

Once your teacher has checked your finished work, keep your CV safe so that you can add to it as you do more and gain more qualifications.

24. Using the CVs of Ryo, Xiao and Su above, answer the following questions.

a. What country does each student come from?

Ryo _____

Xiao _____

Su _____

b. How old is each student?

Ryo _____

Xiao _____

Su _____

c. What activity do they all like? _____

25. Write down three other headings that would be useful in a CV. For example: *Years of schooling in your home country*. Write them down and fill them in on your CV for yourself.

_____

_____

_____

26. It is important that a letter be sent with your CV. Read the letter below as an example.

Write a similar letter, as if you were applying to become a student at a school in New Zealand.

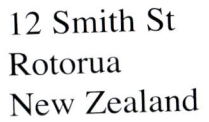

---

12 Smith St
Rotorua
New Zealand

6th February 2003

The Manager
Chicken Heaven
Amohau Street
Rotorua

Dear Sir/madam,

I am a 16 year old student from Thailand and I have been studying English for five years in Thailand. I have received good grades in all my subjects and I would now like to study in a school in New Zealand.

I am a member of my school's drama club and I like playing golf. I would like to continue with both of these interests.

Please let me know what I have to do to apply for a place at your school. I am attaching my CV so you can learn a little bit about me.

You can contact me by fax on 00 662 3476 8971. I look forward to hearing from you.

Yours sincerely,

Pan Thawatchararuk

Pan Thawatchararuk

REVISION

Surname: Ito
First name: Mariko
Nationality: Japanese
School: Auckland Girls' College
Year Level: 10
Age: 16
Phone number: (09) 6735 421

27. Use the ID card to answer the following questions.

a. What is Mariko's nationality?
b. Is Mariko Chinese?
c. Is she a student?
d. What is the area code for her Auckland phone number?
e. What school does Mariko go to?

28. Make up two blank ID cards like the one above, or your teacher may give you a blank copy.

Fill one out for yourself and then fill out the other for another student in the room who you haven't worked with before.

29. Fill the gaps in the sentences below with a verb that makes sense (and is in the correct form).

Example: I *am* a student.

a. I _____ from Korea.
b. My best friend _____ to this school.
c. The teacher _____ late for class.
d. The students in my class _____ noisy.
e. I _____ in a hostel.
f. My friend _____ the Vietnamese language.
g. Our teacher _____ from New Zealand.

30. Fill in the gaps in the letter to make it true for you.

Dear Mum and Dad,

I have now been in New Zealand for _____ months and I am _____ happy at my school and homestay. I _____ in Year _____ at school, and I study English for _____ periods a day. I _____ English lessons! I _____ made some new friends and I _____ busy after school each day. I _____ studying hard. I miss you, and _____ like to come home for a holiday soon.

Love from,

_____

31. What nationality are the people from the following countries?

Example: China *Chinese*

a. Korea   _____
b. Thailand   _____
c. Vietnam   _____
d. Fiji   _____
e. Tonga   _____
f. New Zealand   _____
g. Australia   _____
h. USA   _____

32. Write each sentence out changing the contractions into their full form.

Example: They're from Korea. *They are* from Korea.

a. He's a rugby player.   _____
b. They've got maths next period. _____
c. We've had enough pizza.   _____
d. She's the best student in the class. _____
e. I'll be late for school if you don't hurry up. _____

GRAMMAR

Present simple

The present simple tense has three important uses:

a. To describe a **present state** – a state which exists now or a fact that is generally or always true. For example: *Learning English is difficult. I'm Chinese.*

b. To describe a **present habit** – something we do regularly. For example: *What do you do on Saturdays? I play sport. Does he drink alcohol? No he doesn't.*

c. To describe a **present event**. This is not a common use of the present simple. It is used for something that happens as we are speaking. For example: *I agree that we have made a mistake.*

The form of the present simple is:

I work

You work

We work

They work

He/she/it works

Contractions

Contractions are used in speech and informal writing. They should not be used in formal writing.

Verb: am, is, are, have, has, had, would, will

Contractions: 'm, 's, 're, 've, 's, 'd, 'd, 'll,

Example: I'm, he's, they're, could've, John's, he'd, you'd, you'll

The contraction is added to the end of a word, and is indicated with an apostrophe (').

Possession

An apostrophe is used with a noun to indicate possession. For example: John's cat, the teacher's book.

VOCABULARY

nationality / age / spare / wife / husband / brother / sister / son / daughter / cousin / occupation / curriculum vitae / qualifications / surname / first name / alphabetical order

TAPESCRIPTS

Tapescript 1

My name is Keiko and I am 11 years old. I have two brothers and no sisters. We live with our parents. Their Kiwi names are Victor and Marie.

Tapescript 2

15 18 46 7 70 23 80 100 17 25

Tapescript 3

Person A: My name's William. I am a 16 year old student from China. I am very happy here and I am making lots of friends. I have bought a cell phone and I've had to remember my new number so I can tell people how to contact me. It's 025 806 924.

Person B: Let me introduce myself. My name is Mariko and I'm a Japanese intern teacher working in a New Zealand school. I teach Japanese. This is my first job. I'm only 23 years old. I am living in the school hostel, but my friends can phone me on my cell phone on 027 635 412.

Person C: Hello. I've just arrived in New Zealand and I am younger than most of the other international students. I'm 12 years old and I go to intermediate school. I live with a homestay family and their phone number is, umm ... let me see ... 364 8276. I think that's all. Oh! I forgot. My name is Bayu and I'm from Indonesia.

Unit 2   I Need Help To …

Grammar: Present simple tense: Requests for information and help. *How do I open a bank account? Do I need a passport? How do I get to?* Directions: *walk along/turn left/turn right into.* Bank and post office procedures: *filling in forms/opening accounts/deposits/withdrawals.*

Vocabulary: Words for bank, post office, official procedures: *passport/account/registration.*

STARTER

1. Write the name of the objects in the correct box.

a.
b. 
c. 
d. 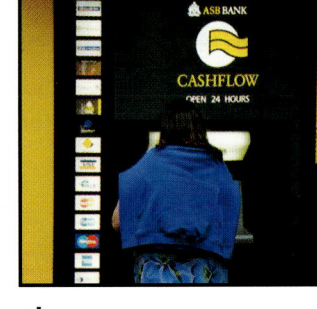
e. 
f. 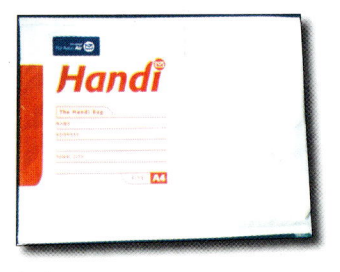

	Bank	Post office
a.		
b.		
c.		
d.		
e.		
f.		

14

Unit 2   i Need Help To...

2. Which of the following things could you post home?

a. chocolate
b. photos
c. bank notes
d. coins
e. school reports
f. your dirty washing

Why don't they make the space bigger?

3. You are going to the bank to open a bank account. What two things must you take with you?

a. _____
b. _____

4. Match the object with its use by drawing a line between them.

envelope	put on an envelope to show postage has been paid
stamp	write a short note on one side
notepaper	put your letter in this
customs declaration	write your letter on this
prepaid envelope	say what is in a parcel for clearance by customs
postcard	an envelope for which postage has already been paid

5. Use your dictionary to write the meanings of the following words.

a. car registration
b. prescription (from a doctor)
c. credit (at a bank)
d. optician
e. cash
f. emergency
g. appointment
h. courier post
i. teller

6. Where do you go if you need to do the following things? Choose a place from the box. Note, some places can be used more than once.

bus station   bank   hairdresser   post office
doctor's surgery or medical clinic   chemist
optician   Vodafone or Telecom office
travel agent

Example: change your money into New Zealand dollars
bank

a. post a parcel _____
b. register a car _____
c. fill a prescription a doctor has given you _____
d. buy a cell phone _____
e. have your eyes tested _____
f. obtain help because you feel unwell _____
g. book your ticket home _____
h. catch a bus to another city _____
i. have a haircut _____

English Zone Elementary Student Book

7. Label the items in the pictures.

a. _____

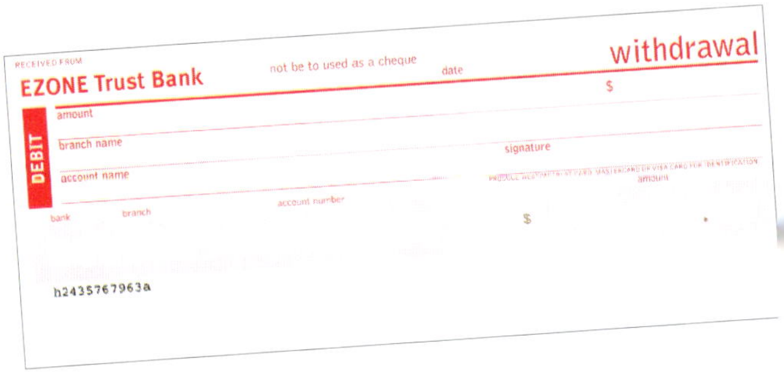

b. _____

c. _____

d. _____

e. _____

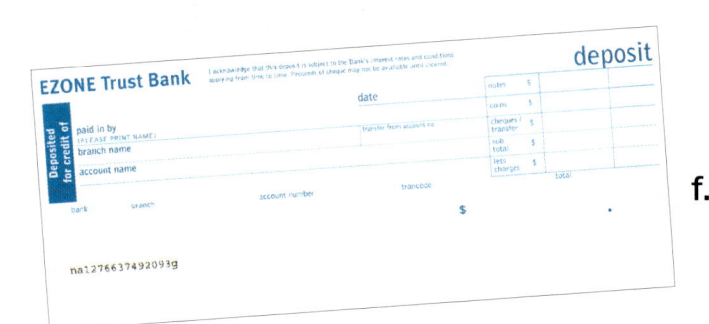

f. _____

g. _____

h. _____

16

Unit 2   i Need Help To...

LISTENING

8. Read the questions below first. Then listen to the tape and answer the questions below. Ask your teacher to replay the tape if you need to hear it again.

In the bank

a. What does a student need in order to open a bank account?
b. What is the information that the student doesn't know?
c. What PIN number does the student want to use?
d. What two things does the bank teller tell the student not to do?
e. What currency is the student's money?
f. What is a cashcard?
g. What information does the student need to write on the cashcard?
h. Why would the student need a cashcard?
i. How many digits are in the PIN number?
j. What is the name of the bank machine?

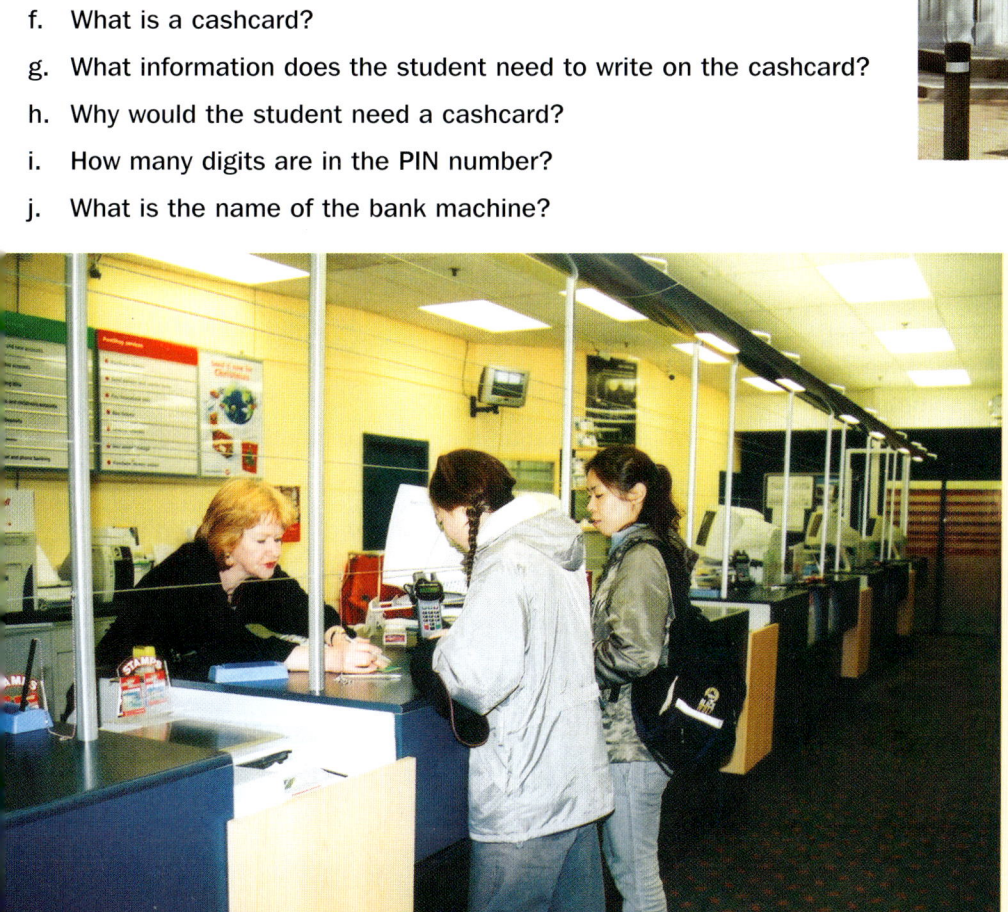

In the post office

a. What is in the student's parcel?
b. Why can't the student send cheese to China?
c. Who will eat the cheese?
d. What will he send instead?

READING and WRITING

What happens to my mail?

New Zealand is a really nice place, but at times I get homesick. Sometimes I really miss my family. My teacher said I should write a letter home to my family. Over the weekend, I wrote a letter asking how they were and if they missed me as well. On Monday morning I went to the teacher and asked her, 'How do I mail this letter home?'

'We place it in an envelope with your parents' address on it, just like you do in China,' she explained. 'It is just like home, but there are postboxes everywhere in New Zealand and you can place your letter in any of them.'

'How many postage stamps do I need to put on?' I asked. She said 'That is a hard question, I don't know, but we can find out if we visit the post office.' Next thing I know she is taking the class on a visit to the post office. All of us! The postmaster explains that the cost of mailing a letter depends on where it is going and its weight. It starts to sound all a little difficult to understand. So I say, 'All I wanted to do was post a letter home,' and the postmaster replied, 'What if one day you want to send something else home which is larger?' He explained, 'You can send almost anything home from the post office.' That started me thinking. I could send home some things from New Zealand so they could see what New Zealand looks like.

My best friend Yomiko asked the postmaster, 'What happens to the letters from here?' I think that was an invitation the postmaster was hoping for. We all got invited out the back to see the mail sorting room. The room was noisy with thousands of letters running along a conveyor belt. They were moving so fast! Yomiko asked, 'How does the machine know which letter goes where, when it is going so fast?' The mail sorter explained. 'When letters have post codes written on the letter clearly, or a barcode if it is a business letter, the machine can read them. If the machine cannot read them, then we sort them by hand. We also sort the parcels and larger letters. The machine stamps each letter with a postmark showing the date, the time and the mail centre. If you look at any letter you have received you will see this information.'

'What happens to them after they are sorted?' said Bill. The postmaster explained. 'They are then placed into these bins for different areas and overseas countries. When the bin is full, the bag is closed and taken to the area by one of our post trucks. If it is going overseas, it is taken to the international airport by an overseas freight company. Sometimes, if you are at the airport you might see the huge freight planes, but sometimes the mail can be on a normal passenger plane.'

'How long will it take to get my letter to Japan?' asked Yomiko. The postmaster said, 'About two days from when you post it. It is then up to your Japanese post office to send it to your home. It could easily take one week.'

'Great,' said Yomiko. 'And what if ...'

'NO!' We all called out to Yomiko, 'No more questions.'

The teacher said, 'I think we have learnt enough about the post office for one day. Thank you and your post office staff very much.'

As we were walking out Yomiko was still looking back to the sorting room. Perhaps we should mail Yomiko to Japan and then she would see how the mail goes, first hand!

9. Answer the following questions using information from the passage above.

a. Why are the letters postmarked?

b. Where does the postmark go?

c. What information is on the postmark?

d. How are the letters sorted?

e. Where do the letters go after they have been sorted?

f. How are the letters delivered overseas?

g. How long might it take a letter to reach Japan?

h. What is a postcode?

Visit <www.post.co.nz> for more information on NZ Post.

Unit 2   i Need Help To...

10. Read and fill out the *Just to let you know we're moving* form, using your own name and address.

Just to let you know we're moving

Name:
Customer number:
Our/my old address was:

Our/my new address is:

New telephone/s:

Signature:
If you wish to include confidential information we suggest you enclose this card in an envelope.

New address effective from:

New Zealand Post

Postage Included

Note: postage included within New Zealand and overseas.

To:

11. You are posting a gift of a book of New Zealand photos to your parents. It is worth $50. Fill in the customs declaration form using your name and address.

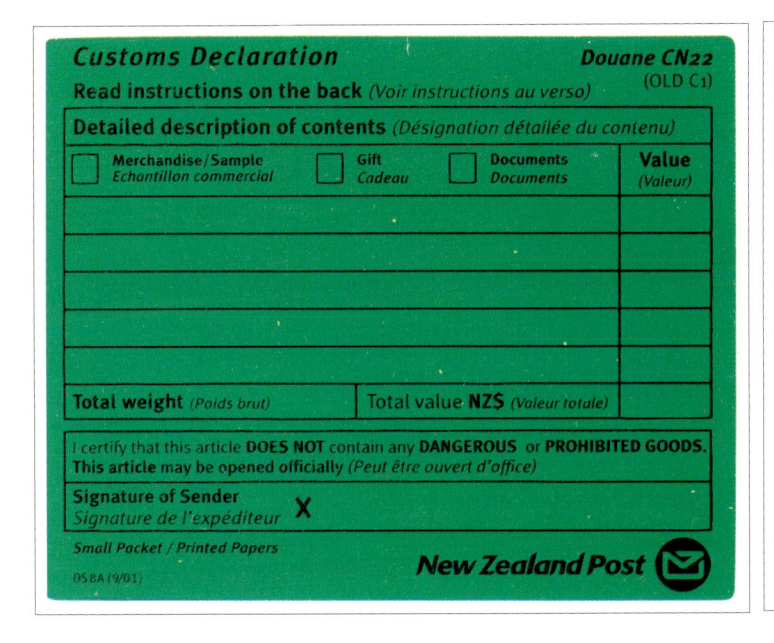

Customs Declaration   *Douane CN22*
(OLD C1)
Read instructions on the back *(Voir instructions au verso)*
Detailed description of contents *(Désignation détaillée du contenu)*

☐ Merchandise/Sample *Echantillon commercial*	☐ Gift *Cadeau*	☐ Documents *Documents*	Value *(Valeur)*

Total weight *(Poids brut)*   Total value NZ$ *(Valeur totale)*

I certify that this article **DOES NOT** contain any **DANGEROUS** or **PROHIBITED GOODS**. This article may be opened officially *(Peut être ouvert d'office)*

Signature of Sender
Signature de l'expéditeur   X

Small Packet / Printed Papers
058A (9/01)

New Zealand Post

Instructions

If the value of the contents exceeds NZ$620.00 a red CN23 customs declaration should be completed.

1. The contents of your item (even if a gift or sample) must be described fully and accurately. Non-observance of this condition may lead to delay of the item and inconvenience to the addressee, or even lead to the seizure of the item by the customs authorities abroad.

2. Please indicate the value of each item in your package and the total value of your package.

    Your item must not contain dangerous or prohibited goods eg: cash, explosives, flammables, aerosols. If in doubt ask at any Post Shop.

    * A false declaration is a criminal offence
    * This item may be opened officially

English Zone Elementary Student Book

APPLICATION

12. Listen to Tapescript 3. Fill in the gaps for the instructions below.

a.

Student Excuse me, I have a prescription. Is _____ a chemist _____ here?

Person Yes. Keep walking down _____ _____ and it is on your right, on the corner of _____ Street.

b.

Student I would like to _____ my tickets home. Is there a _____ _____ near here?

Person Yes, walk down _____ _____ and turn _____ at Princess Street. The travel agent is on your _____.

c.

Student I need to _____ a bank account. Is _____ a bank near here?

Person There are _____. One on the next corner, and the other opposite the _____ on Princess Street.

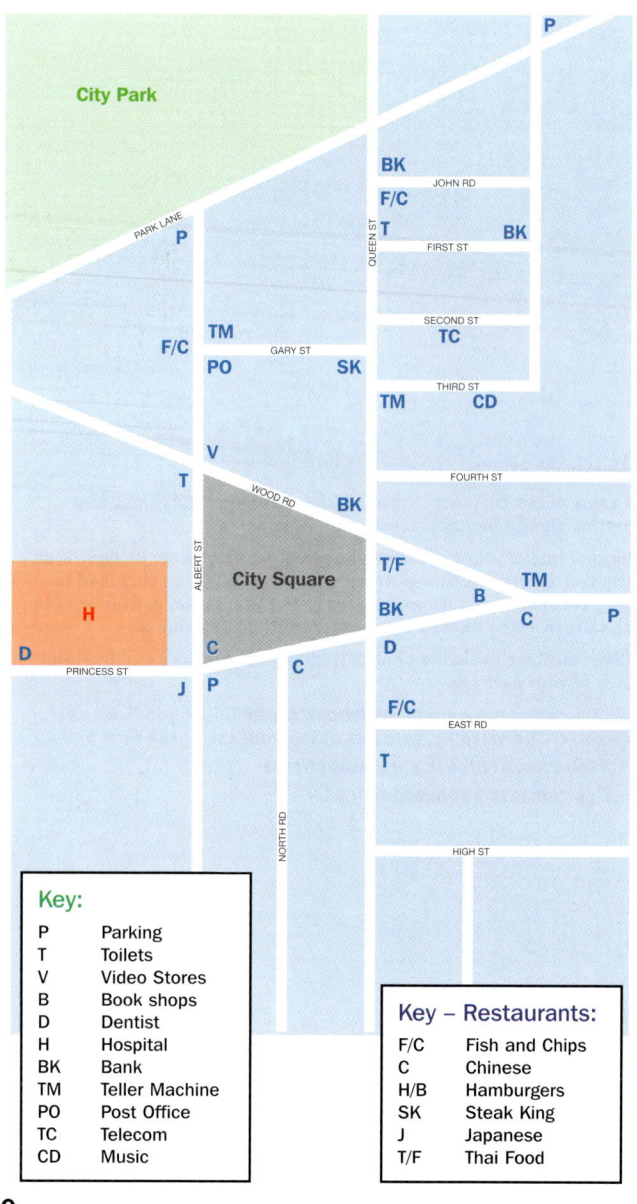

13. Use the map and say where you would go in the following situations.

Example: You want to buy a cheap gift for a small child.
The $2 shop on Albert Sreet

a. want to hire a video
_____

b. want to buy a dictionary
_____

c. want to withdraw some money but the banks are closed
_____

d. feel hungry and want some Chinese food
_____

e. feel hungry and want a hamburger and some chips
_____

f. have a toothache and need help
_____

g. want to post a letter
_____

h. need a new SIM card for your cell phone
_____

i. want to buy a CD you have seen advertised
_____

Key:
P — Parking
T — Toilets
V — Video Stores
B — Book shops
D — Dentist
H — Hospital
BK — Bank
TM — Teller Machine
PO — Post Office
TC — Telecom
CD — Music

Key – Restaurants:
F/C — Fish and Chips
C — Chinese
H/B — Hamburgers
SK — Steak King
J — Japanese
T/F — Thai Food

14. Fill in the gaps using the words listed in the box.

> OK   PIN   amount   account   money   card

Instructions for withdrawing money using your ATM card.

Example: Put your *card* into the slot in the machine.

a. Put in your _____ number.

b. Select the service you want (withdrawal) and the _____ you want to use.

c. Key in the _____ you want to withdraw.

d. Confirm by pressing _____.

e. Remove your _____.

f. Collect the _____.

15. All motor vehicles in New Zealand need to be licensed due to the Transport Act 1986.

If you purchase a car you will need to send change of ownership details to the Transport Registry Centre. When purchasing a car, ensure that it has a current Warrant of Fitness and is registered.

Fill out the Application to License Motor Vehicle form supplied by your teacher. Assume you are changing the ownership on the following car to yourself for private use.

Type of car: Renault

Registration plate number: REN 000

Colour: blue with a yellow stripe

English Zone Elementary Student Book

REVISION

18. When do you need to use a Customs Declaration Form?

_____

_____

19. Complete these details about yourself.

Given name: _____

First name: _____

Middle name: _____

Full name: _____

Last name: _____

Surname: _____

Family name: _____

20. Place the following statements in the correct order by putting the letters a. to h. in front of each sentence.

a.   Place the mailing address on the envelope.

____ The Chinese post office then sends the letter to my home.

____ It may take a week to get from New Zealand to home.

____ It is taken to the airport.

____ Post the envelope into a postbox.

____ It is air freighted to my home country, China.

____ The envelope is sorted by the post office sorting machine.

____ Place a stamp in the right hand corner.

16. Collect a copy of the bank application form from your teacher and fill in as many details for yourself as you can.

Complete the form for yourself only unless you share a bank account with someone else.

17. Which of the following things could you post home?

a. computer program

b. photos

c. food

d. money

e. school reports

f. clothes

21. Explain to a partner how a letter finds its way from you to home.

Use the statements above in your discussion. Did you change the wording of the statements when you said them? Ask another student to listen to what you said and write out any changes that you _made_.
For example: I _wrote_ the mailing address ...

GRAMMAR

Requests

To ask someone to do something for you, use one of the following forms.

Please *can / will / would / could* you plus the verb.

For example: Please *can you help me mail* this letter?
Please *could you help me find* the post office?

Directions

To give spoken directions you need to tell someone exactly what to do in detail. For example: *Turn right/left at the end of the road. Go straight until you get to the church, and then continue along the road until you reach the station.*

VOCABULARY

passport / account / ATM machine / ATM card / digit / customs / deposit / withdrawal / prepaid / envelope / prescription / optician / appointment / emergency / car registration / currency / left / right / opposite / next to

TAPESCRIPTS

Tapescript 1

Bankteller (BT) Next please.

Student (St) I'd like to open a bank account please.

BT OK. Have you got your passport and some money to deposit? You need a minimum of NZ$500 to open an account.

St Yes, here's my passport and $250 in US currency.

BT Good. Now you need to fill in this form with your name, passport number, local address and phone number.

St Oh! Sorry I don't know my homestay's phone number.

BT That's OK. You can put your cell phone number and we will also record your school's number for an emergency contact.

St Done! Is this alright?

BT Yes. Now, do you want a cashcard as well? You will need a card if you want to withdraw money during the times the bank isn't open.

St Yes please.

BT Right. I just need to complete these forms and deposit your money. Then I will show you how to use the card. Please sign the card here. You will need to choose a PIN number.

St Can I use my birthday?

BT No, that's not a good idea. Choose another less common four-digit number, but don't tell me what it is.

St Right, I've got one.

BT Good. Now enter the numbers into this little computer. Thanks. Put them in again just to double check the number. Now, come with me out to the ATM machine and we will practise using you card.

Tapescript 2

Post Office Assistant (POA) Can I help you?

Student (St) I'd like to send this parcel to my parents in China.

POA OK. What's in the parcel?

St It's NZ cheese.

POA I'm sorry. I don't think that Customs in both NZ and China will allow you to post cheese. Also it would go off during the travelling time.

St Oh no! I really wanted my parents to taste it. I guess I will have to give it to my homestay mother.

POA Perhaps you can send a book about New Zealand food to your parents.

St Good idea. Thank you.

Tapescript 3

a.
Student Excuse me. I have a prescription. Is there a chemist near here?

Person Yes. Keep walking down Queen Street and it is on your right, on the corner of Princess Street.

b.
Student I would like to book my tickets home. Is there a travel agent near here?

Person Yes, walk down Queen Street and turn right at Princess Street. The travel agent is on your left.

c.
Student I need to open a bank account. Is there a bank near here?

Person There are two. One on the next corner, and the other is opposite the chemist on Princess Street.

Unit 3   I'm Feeling Good ... I Think?

Grammar: Describing health problems: *I have a headache. I cannot see.* Giving advice: *You shouldn't/You'd better not.*

Vocabulary: Parts of the body, medical terms and personnel.

STARTER

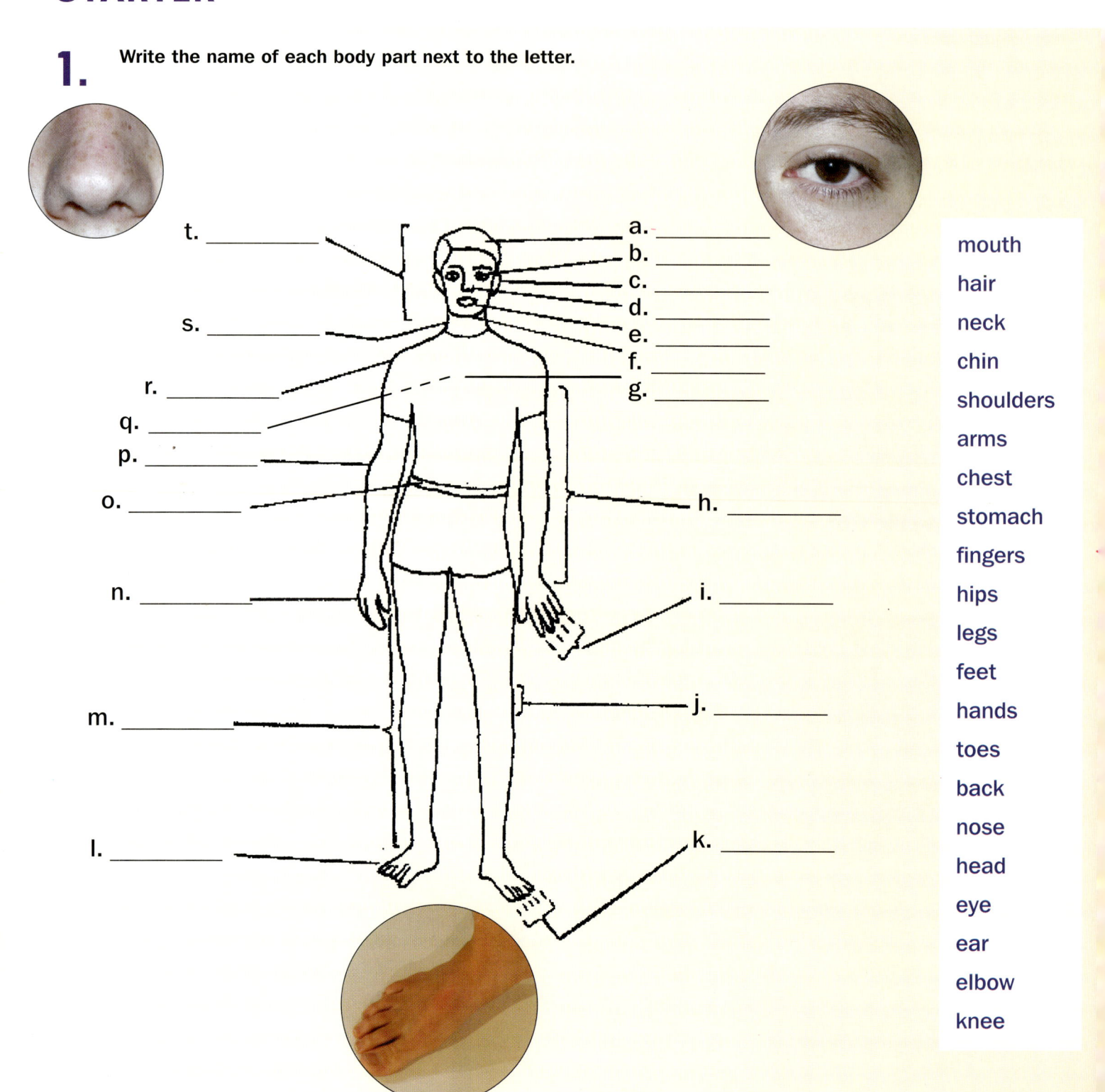

1. Write the name of each body part next to the letter.

t. _____
s. _____
r. _____
q. _____
p. _____
o. _____
n. _____
m. _____
l. _____

a. _____
b. _____
c. _____
d. _____
e. _____
f. _____
g. _____
h. _____
i. _____
j. _____
k. _____

mouth
hair
neck
chin
shoulders
arms
chest
stomach
fingers
hips
legs
feet
hands
toes
back
nose
head
eye
ear
elbow
knee

24

Unit 3   I'm Feeling Good ... I Think?

c. How many more bones does a baby have than an adult?

d. When are all people colour-blind?

e. Where does your food go if you are standing on your head?

f. What is the largest organ of your body?

2. Write down a description of each of the people in the photo.

For example: *He has black hair. She has blonde hair.* Use some of the following adjectives.

small big tall short long blue brown black thin fat blonde

3. Read the following information and then answer the questions.

- More than half the bones in the body are in the hands and feet.
- The heart beats 3 billion times in an average person's lifetime.
- A newborn baby has 350 bones. A fully grown adult has only 206.
- Everyone is colour-blind at birth.
- Food will get to your stomach even if you stand on your head.
- Skin is the largest organ of the body.

a. What parts of your body contain half your bones?

b. How many times does an average person's heart beat in their lifetime?

4. Label each picture with one of the phrases from the list below.

He's cut his hand.

He's got a toothache.

He's got a cold.

She's got a sore leg.

She's got a headache.

a. _____

b. _____

c. _____

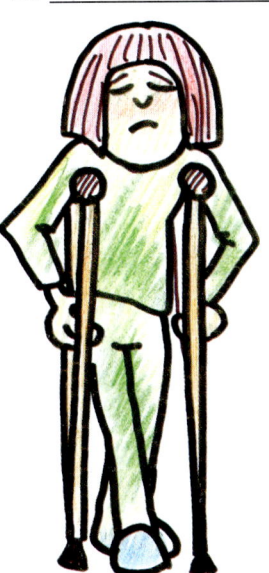

d. _____

e. _____

25

5. Divide the foods and activities in the box into healthy and unhealthy.

chocolate fruit vegetables meat cake
ice-cream white bread wholemeal bread
walking running watching TV internet games
playing sports

Healthy	Unhealthy

7. List the foods you would like to eat if you decided you wanted to eat a healthier diet.

_____
_____
_____
_____
_____
_____

6. Write whether the food in each picture is healthy or unhealthy.

a.  _____   b. _____

c.  _____   d. _____

e.  _____   f. _____

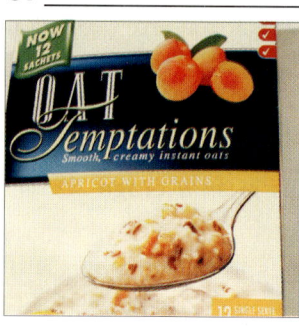

g. 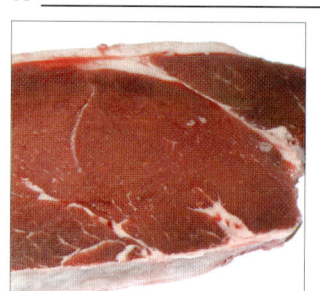 _____   h. _____

i. _____

Unit 3   I'm Feeling Good ... I Think?

LISTENING

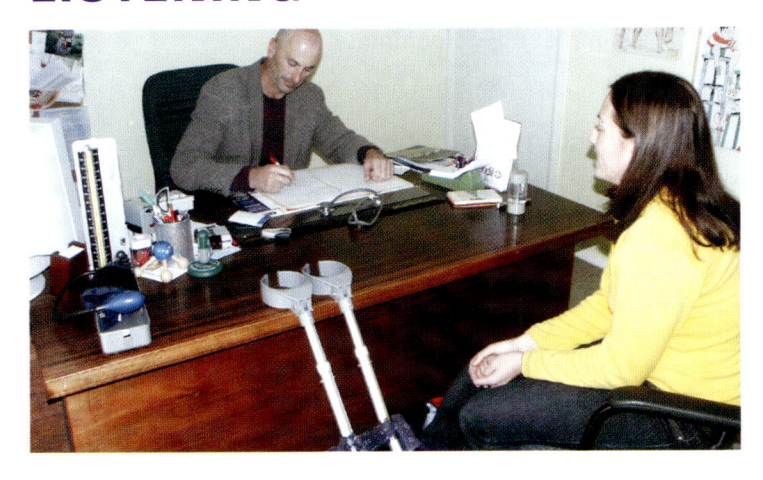

8. Listen to Tapescript 1 and then answer the questions.

a. What is wrong with each patient?

Carrie _____

Seok _____

Mrs Brown _____

b. What does the doctor tell each patient to do?

Carrie _____

Seok _____

Mrs Brown _____

9. Listen to Tapescript 2 and then write down what the student *has* to do, and the other things he *wants* to do.

10. Listen to Tapescript 3 and answer the questions.

a. Why has the student come to the gym?

b. What type of exercise does the gym instructor talk about?

c. What will he have to do in addition to exercising?

d. What will the instructor do before he/she develops a program for the student?

e. When will the student start his program?

SPEAKING

11. Role-plays

a. Collect a role-play card from your teacher and act out the situations it describes with a partner.

Use the following phrases:

I can't …

I've got …

You should …

You shouldn't …

I'll …

You'd better …

b. Collect a second role-play card and find a new partner to act out the situation on this card.

12. Collect an Emergency Department role-play card from your teacher. Find a new partner and act out the role-play.

27

English Zone Elementary Student Book

READING

Read the poem to yourself as you listen to the tape.

Willie's Wart

Willie had a stubborn wart
upon his middle toe.
Regardless, though, of what he tried
the wart refused to go.

So Willie went and visited
his family foot physician,
who instantly agreed
it was a stubborn wart condition.

The doctor tried to squeeze the wart.
He tried to twist and turn it.
He tried to scrape and shave the wart.
He tried to boil and burn it.

He poked it with a pair of tongs.
He pulled it with his tweezers.
He held it under heat lamps
and he crammed it into freezers.

Regrettably these treatments
were of very little use.
He looked at it and sputtered,
'Ach! I cannot get it loose!'

'I'll have to get some bigger tools
to help me to dissect it.
I'll need to pound and pummel it,
bombard it and inject it.'

He whacked it with a hammer
and he yanked it with a wrench.
He seared it with a welding torch
despite the nasty stench.

He drilled it with a power drill.
He wrestled it with pliers.
He zapped it with a million volts
from large electric wires.

He blasted it with gamma rays,
besieged it with corrosives,
assaulted it with dynamite
and nuclear explosives.

He hit the wart with everything
but when the smoke had cleared,
poor Willie's stubborn wart remained,
and Willie'd disappeared.
by Linda Knaus and Kenn Nesbitt

13. Find pairs of words in the box that mean the same.
Example: *physician/doctor*

> physician / stubborn / cram / dissect / pummel / bombard / whack / yank / stench / corrosive / assault / sear / strike / obstinate / bash / cut up / burn / attack / doctor / bad smell / force / smash / acid / pull

14. Put these same words into the following table identifying nouns, adjectives, and verbs.

	Nouns	Adjectives	Verbs
Example:	*physician*	*stubborn*	*cram*

15. Tell a partner what happened to poor Willie in your own words. Use some of the new words you have learnt in this poem.

16. Read the poem again and answer the questions.

a. Why did Willie go to the doctor?
_____

b. What is a welding torch usually used for?
_____

c. List all the unusual tools that the doctor used.
_____

d. What was the final result of the visit to the doctor?
_____

WRITING

17. Write advice for the following problems.

Example:
Problem: I have put on a lot of weight in New Zealand.

Solution: *You shouldn't eat so much junk food.*

a. Problem: I have a sore tooth

   Solution: *You should* _____
   _____

b. Problem: I can't see the board at school.

   Solution: *You should* _____
   _____
   _____

c. Problem: I hurt my foot playing football.

   Solution: _____
   _____
   _____

d. Problem: I've got a cold.

   Solution: _____
   _____
   _____

18. Collect a Medical History form from your teacher and fill in the details.

It would be a good idea to keep a copy of this form in case you need to go to the hospital or a doctor for treatment.

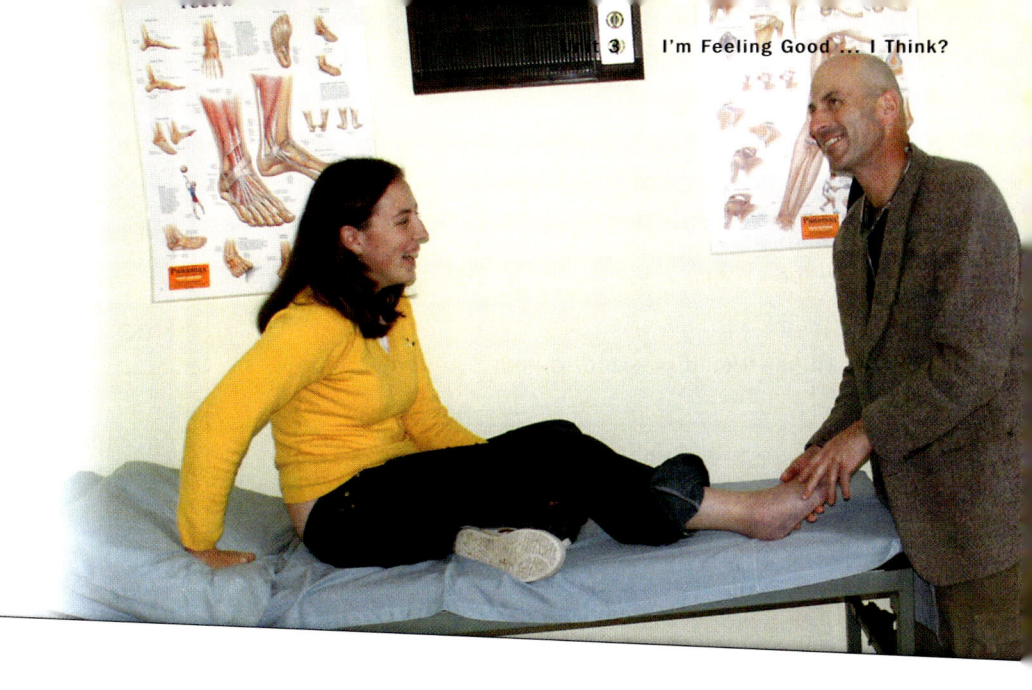

I'm Feeling Good ... I Think?

Medical History
Confidential (For record purposes and pre-treatment evaluation)

NAME _____ D.O.B. _____
      Surname   First Names   Mr, Mrs, Ms

ADDRESS (Home) _____
         (Bus) _____
OCCUPATION _____
TELEPHONE (Home) _____ (Bus) _____
PARTNER'S NAME _____
    Occupation _____
NAME OF DOCTOR _____
ADDRESS_____
REFERRED BY _____ PHONE _____

1. Have you been a patient in a hospital?
   Reason _____ Yes/No

2. Are you, or have you recently been, under the care of a doctor?
   Reason _____ Yes/No

3. Have you taken any medicine or drugs during the past year?
   Details _____ Yes/No

4. Have you ever experienced any ill effects from penicillin, sleeping tablets, local anaesthetics or any other drugs?
   Details _____ Yes/No

5. Circle the name of any of the following which you have had: HEART TROUBLE, HIGH BLOOD PRESSURE, RHEUMATIC FEVER, Asthma, Diabetes, Arthritis, Persistent Cough or Bronchitis, Jaundice or Hepatitis, Ulcer, Anaemia, Sinusitis, Allergy (describe type).
   _____

6. Have you had any other serious illness?
   Details _____ Yes/No

7. Women: If pregnant, please state the number of months: _____

8. I authorise any person or company to provide you or your nominees with such information about me as you may require in regard to request for credit. I authorise you to furnish to any third party details of certain information held by you for the purposes of administration and protection of such credit.

DATE _____ SIGNATURE _____

English Zone Elementary Student Book

APPLICATION

19. You have decided to change your life and become a fitter, healthier individual.

a. What things would you take out of your daily diet?

_____

b. What things would you add to your daily diet?

_____

c. Fill out the diary page with your activities for an average day that would give you a balance between work, exercise and recreation.

Tuesday 20th

My healthier lifestyle

7.30am   Get up and have breakfast.

8am   Walk to school

20. In groups, discuss why it is important to eat healthy food and exercise regularly.

Make a list of at least *five* healthy activities and reasons why they are healthy. One student from each group will report back to the class.

Healthy activity	Health benefit
Eat more dairy products	calcium strengthens bones

21. Match the problems with the person you would go to for advice by drawing a line between them.

a bad cold	teacher
toothache	doctor
schoolwork is too hard	dentist
feeling very homesick	homestay mother
NZ food is making you sick	counsellor/dean

Unit 3   I'm Feeling Good ... I Think?

22. Find a partner and tell them about a real or imaginary problem that you have.

Your partner will give you some advice. Then change roles and listen to your partner's problem and give them some advice.

> I have a very bad cold. My throat is sore and my head is blocked.

> You should visit the local doctor.

23. Write a letter to a problem page in a magazine. Swap with a friend and write answers to the problems raised.

Example:

Dear Dorothy, I have a headache. Thanks X. Reply: Dear X, You should take some Panadol and if the ache doesn't go away see your doctor.

dear dorothy

Dear Dorothy,
I am from China and I do not like the food my homestay mother gives me for dinner. I don't want to tell her because she will be upset.
Thanks, Hungry

Dear Hungry,
Your homestay family wants you to enjoy your time in New Zealand so it is better to let them know you have a problem eating some of their normal food. You could offer to cook the family a meal that's like one your mother would cook for you.

REVISION

24. When do we use the following things?

a. sticking plaster   _____
b. paracetamol   _____
c. bandage   _____
d. thermometer   _____
e. crutches   _____

25. Label the face using the words from the box.

hair   eye   eyebrow   eyelashes   nose   lips
teeth   chin   ears

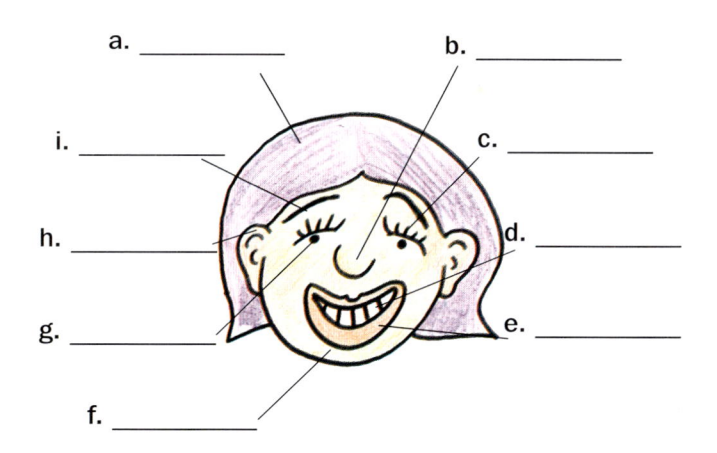

a. _____   b. _____
i. _____   c. _____
h. _____   d. _____
g. _____   e. _____
f. _____

26. What should each of these people do?

Problem	Treatment
a. broken leg	
b. difficulty reading the blackboard	
c. bleeding from a cut	
d. bad headache	
e. bad stomach ache	

English Zone Elementary Student Book

27. Label each of the items in the pictures.

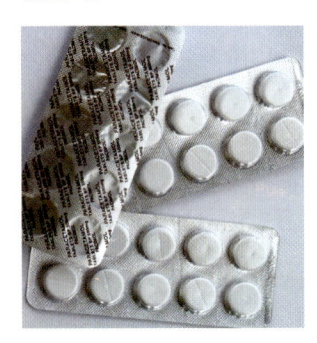

a. _____

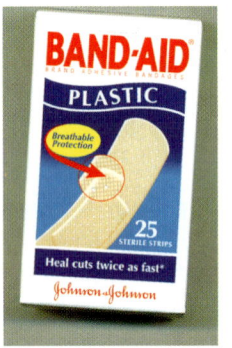

b. _____

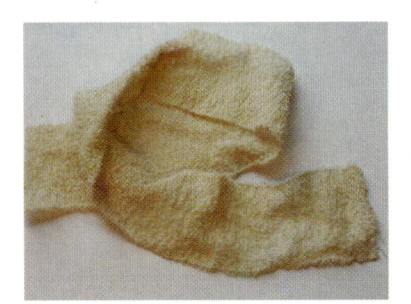

c. _____

d. _____

e. _____

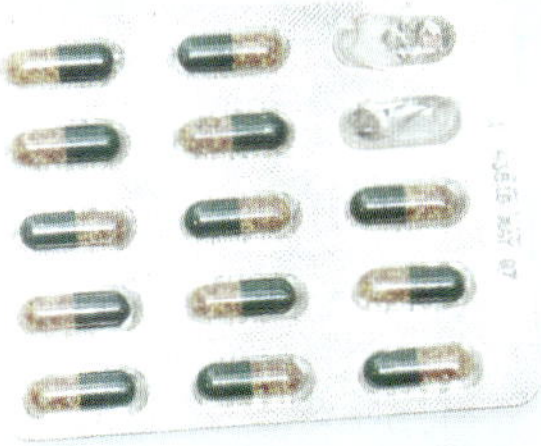

f. _____

GRAMMAR

Giving advice

When you give someone advice, the following phrases are useful: *You'd better …, You'd better not …, You should …, You shouldn't …*

For example: I have a bad headache. *You should see a doctor.* I am late for school. *You'd better hurry or the teacher will be angry.*

Describing problems

When describing a medical problem the verb *to have* is used. We can also use *have got*. For example: *I've got a bad headache*, or *I have a bad headache*.

The verb to have in this context indicates a state of being: have a cold, have the measles, have a stomach ache.

This use of *to have* is also used for other states. For example: *to have an idea, to have two arms and two legs.*

VOCABULARY

eyes / mouth / ears / face / hair / shoulders / arms / hands / fingers / stomach / hips / legs / back / feet / toes / thin / fat / heart / bones / sore throat / X-ray / diarrhoea / vomit / dentist / doctor

TAPESCRIPTS

Tapescript 1a

Doctor Come in. How are you today?

Carrie I've got a sore throat and a runny nose. I feel cold and shivery.

Doctor Oh dear. Let me take a look down your throat. Say Ahhhhh!

Carrie Ahhhhh!

Doctor Mmm. Your throat's a bit red. You're very hot aren't you? It's just a cold I think. You better take some paracetamol and rest for a couple of days.

Tapescript 1b

Doctor Come in. What have you done to your leg?

Soek I was playing tennis and I tripped and fell.

Doctor It's very swollen, and you obviously can't walk on it. I think you better have an X-ray before I do anything else. I'll ask my nurse to organise it for you.

Tapescript 1c

Doctor Good morning Mrs Brown. What can I do for you today?

Mrs Brown I went out for dinner last night, and I've been vomiting and have had diarrhoea since midnight.

Doctor Goodness! Where did you go?

Mrs Brown To a new restaurant on George Street.

Doctor Mm! I'll give you something to stop the vomiting and diarrhoea, but you ought to phone the restaurant and tell them.

Mrs Brown I will, even though I don't feel well. I would hate anyone else to get sick.

Tapescript 2

Teacher You don't look well Jong. You're very pale and your eyes are red. Why did you come to school today?

Jong I've an assignment due in today and I needed to hand it in. I also want to go to the concert in period 4.

Teacher You could have got an extension on your assignment or asked a friend to hand it in for you.

Jong Yes, but then I would have missed the concert in period 4.

Teacher Mm! I understand what you are saying Jong, but there are times when it is better for you if you stay at home and recover, and better for other people as they don't catch your bugs!

Tapescript 3

Gym Instructor (GI) I understand that you want to lose weight and develop your muscles.

Student (St) Yes! I would like to be fitter and I would like bigger muscles.

GI You will need to combine exercise and diet to do that. I will work out a fitness program for you and give you some diet information.

St OK. What type of exercise will I have to do?

GI You will need to combine some aerobic exercises and some weight work in order to develop your muscles and increase your level of fitness.

St Can I start now?

GI I will run you through some fitness tests now, and check your level of fitness and health, and then I will work out a program for you. It will be ready for you next time you come.

Tapescript 4

Willie's Wart

by Linda Knaus and Kenn Nesbitt

Willie had a stubborn wart
upon his middle toe.
Regardless, though, of what he tried
the wart refused to go.

So Willie went and visited
his family foot physician,
who instantly agreed
it was a stubborn wart condition.

The doctor tried to squeeze the wart.
He tried to twist and turn it.
He tried to scrape and shave the wart.
He tried to boil and burn it.

He poked it with a pair of tongs.
He pulled it with his tweezers.
He held it under heat lamps
and he crammed it into freezers.

Regrettably these treatments
were of very little use.
He looked at it and sputtered,
'Ach!, I cannot get it loose!'

'I'll have to get some bigger tools
to help me to dissect it.
I'll need to pound and pummel it,
bombard it and inject it.'

He whacked it with a hammer
and he yanked it with a wrench.
He seared it with a welding torch
despite the nasty stench.

He drilled it with a power drill.
He wrestled it with pliers.
He zapped it with a million volts
from large electric wires.

He blasted it with gamma rays,
besieged it with corrosives,
assaulted it with dynamite
and nuclear explosives.

He hit the wart with everything
but when the smoke had cleared,
poor Willie's stubborn wart remained,
and Willie'd disappeared.

Unit 4 Exploring New Zealand

Grammar: Ability and permission: *can/can't*. Likes and dislikes revised.
Vocabulary: New Zealand place names: *Bay of Islands, Kaikoura*. Tourist attractions: *bungy jumping/whale watching*.

STARTER

Queenstown is situated in Central Otago in the South Island. It has a beautiful lake (Lake Wakatipu) and is surrounded by mountain ranges. It is well known for tourist activities such as skiing, bungy jumping, goldmining, jet-boat rides, white-water rafting and many others.

Kaikoura is two and a half hours from Christchurch in the South Island of New Zealand. It is known for whale watching, swimming with dolphins, trout and salmon fishing, and coastal walks.

Christchurch is the largest city in the South Island and is situated in Canterbury. It is New Zealand's 'garden city' and is well known for its beautiful parks and gardens. Tourist attractions include tram rides, wildlife reserves, the Antarctic Centre, a casino, Science Alive, and a number of beautiful buildings housing galleries and museums.

Wellington is the capital city of New Zealand and is situated at the southern most end of the North Island. Parliament is housed there in the famous 'Beehive' and it is the centre of New Zealand commerce and politics. Wellington is the home of the country's national museum, Te Papa.

Taupo is situated by New Zealand's largest lake, in the central North Island. Lake Taupo was created by a volcanic eruption approximately 2000 years ago. Taupo is known for its hot pools, water sports, bungy jumping, the Huka Falls, bushwalks and geothermal areas.

Rotorua is situated about 45 minutes north of Taupo in the central North Island. It is known for its geothermal activity, Maori arts and crafts, Mount Tarawera and the Buried Village, water sports on the lakes and bushwalks in the surrounding forest areas.

The Bay of Islands is situated to the north of the North Island and is made up of 140 islands with Paihia as the main centre for visitors. The Bay of Islands is known for its sightseeing cruises, water sports, whale watching, swimming with dolphins, and for the historical setting of Russell, where the Treaty of Waitangi was signed.

Unit 4 Exploring New Zealand

1. With your teacher and other students identify where the following places are on the map.

a. the Bay of Islands
b. Auckland
c. Rotorua
d. Taupo
e. Wellington
f. Kaikoura
g. Christchurch
h. Queenstown

2. Use the map and the surrounding information to answer the following questions.

a. Where is Queenstown?
b. Where is Paihia?
c. What other tourist centre is close to Rotorua?
d. Which is the 'garden city' of New Zealand?
e. Where can you whale watch and swim with the dolphins?
f. Where was the Treaty of Waitangi signed?
g. Which lake is the result of a volcanic eruption 2000 years ago?
h. What is the capital city of New Zealand?

3. Based on the information around the map write the following activities on to the locations where they can be done.

a. skiing
b. sightseeing cruises
c. whale watching
d. riding a tram
e. sailing
f. white-water rafting
g. bungy jumping
h. visit the Buried Village
i. visit the Beehive
j. see the Huka Falls

35

LISTENING

4. Listen to Tapescript 1 of people talking about places they have visited in New Zealand.

Read the task below and listen carefully to the tape again, then complete the following table for each person.

Places I visited in New Zealand

	Person A	Person B	Person C
a. Where did they visit?			
b. What can tourists do there?			
c. What did they see?			
d. What did they like and dislike?			

5. Listen to the conversation between the receptionist and the student on Tapescript 2 and then answer the following questions.

a. What is the cheapest holiday option?
b. How much does it cost per day?
c. What meal will he have to pay for himself?
d. Why couldn't he book for the Sunday trip?
e. How will he travel from Wellington to Picton?
f. What time does the ferry leave Wellington for Picton?
g. When does the tour bus leave the ferry terminal?
h. What is the total cost of the trip?
i. What day did he book?

6. Listen to the tape again for the names of the places visited. Write down the places mentioned.

_____
_____
_____
_____
_____

READING/WRITING

Prereading activity

This brochure was written for adult tourists. It contains some difficult words that may be used in general tourist brochures and terms that describe yachts and yacht races. The following words and their meanings will help you understand the brochure.

Word	Meaning
charter	to hire or to rent
energetic	full of energy
grand prix	major race
grinders	people on yacht who wind in the winches
participate	to join in and be involved
prestigious	recognised as important by many people
professional	experienced, trained and capable
regatta	yacht racing carnival
skipper	captain, the person in charge
syndicate	a group of business people
ultimate	the best possible, unbeatable
winches	a winding machine used to tighten ropes
yachty	sailor

America's Cup Sailing...

The America's Cup is the world's oldest and most prestigious sporting trophy and ultimate yachting regatta. Team New Zealand is the previous holder of the America's Cup and is working hard to keep ahead of syndicates funded by some of the world's richest billionaires. In Auckland the public have a unique opportunity to participate in sailing one of these grand prix race boats usually reserved for only the most elite yacht racers.

NZL40 was originally built by Challenge du Yacht Club Antibes for the 1995 America's Cup in San Diego. It was not finished in time so did not race but was completed in 1998 and brought to New Zealand as a trial boat for the 1999–2000 America's Cup in Auckland. NZL40 is the 40th America's Cup yacht built to the international America's Cup Class (ACC) rule that was first used in San Diego 1992. Constructed of carbon fibre and other high tech materials NZL40 cost approximately $3.5 million dollars to build.

In January 2000 a local Auckland company, Viking Cruises, bought NZL40 to take passengers sailing, and has changed the boat as little as possible. NZL40 is now recognised as the official America's Cup charter yacht for the America's Cup 2003 and will continue giving passengers a very real America's Cup experience. The passengers become the crew and are encouraged to participate in the sailing, however some may rather sit back and watch the action leaving the hard work to the more energetic grinders.

The trip suits people of all experiences and abilities and is a once in a lifetime opportunity. Our professional skipper and crew are keen racing yachties and will ensure you get the most out of your two hour sail onboard NZL40.

Visit <www.sailnewzealand.co.nz> for more information.

7. Read all the information on the brochure and answer the questions.

a. How much did NZL40 cost to build?
b. When was NZL40 completed?
c. What is NZL40 used for now?
d. What is a charter yacht?
e. Who are the crew when you ride on this yacht?
f. Who does the trip suit?
g. How long does the trip take?
h. How do you book a trip on the yacht?

8. Assume you visit the website <www.sailnewzealand.co.nz> and like what you read.

You want to book a trip on the yacht for yourself and two friends. Write an email covering the following points:

a. Say when you want to sail.
b. Tell them the number of tickets you want.
c. Ask how much it will cost.
d. Ask how experienced you have to be.
e. Say how you can be contacted.

9. Assume you have now returned from your trip on NZL40.

The weather was fine and the water quite calm. The boat took 10 passengers and you all worked as crew. You were on the water for two hours and saw a lot of other sailing boats on the harbour. You enjoyed the trip and would like to sail again. Write a letter to your parents telling them about your trip.

10. Read the information about the Granary Backpackers Hostel and write a letter or email to book accommodation for three people. Include the following:

a. What type of room you want.
b. Ask how you can get to the city centre from the hostel and how long it would take.
c. Ask whether you can cook your own meals in the rooms.
d. The dates you are going to need accommodation.
e. How many people require accommodation.

http://www.yachtbackers.co.nz

Search: Accommodation

Granary Backpackers Hostel

123 Park Road, Auckland, 1001

Phone/fax: 09 809 5777

Large historic house overlooking the harbour and near museum and botanic gardens. Twin, double, shared rooms available. Private courtyard with swimming pool, fitness centre and barbeque area. Bike and luggage storage, mail and messages held, car hire arranged, 24-hour airport transport, off-street parking, travel information. Walk to the city centre with its shops, cafes, pubs and entertainment.

Email: yachtbackers@xtra.co.nz

Web: www.yachtbackers.co.nz

All rates are GST inclusive unless otherwise noted.

Unit 4   Exploring New Zealand

SPEAKING

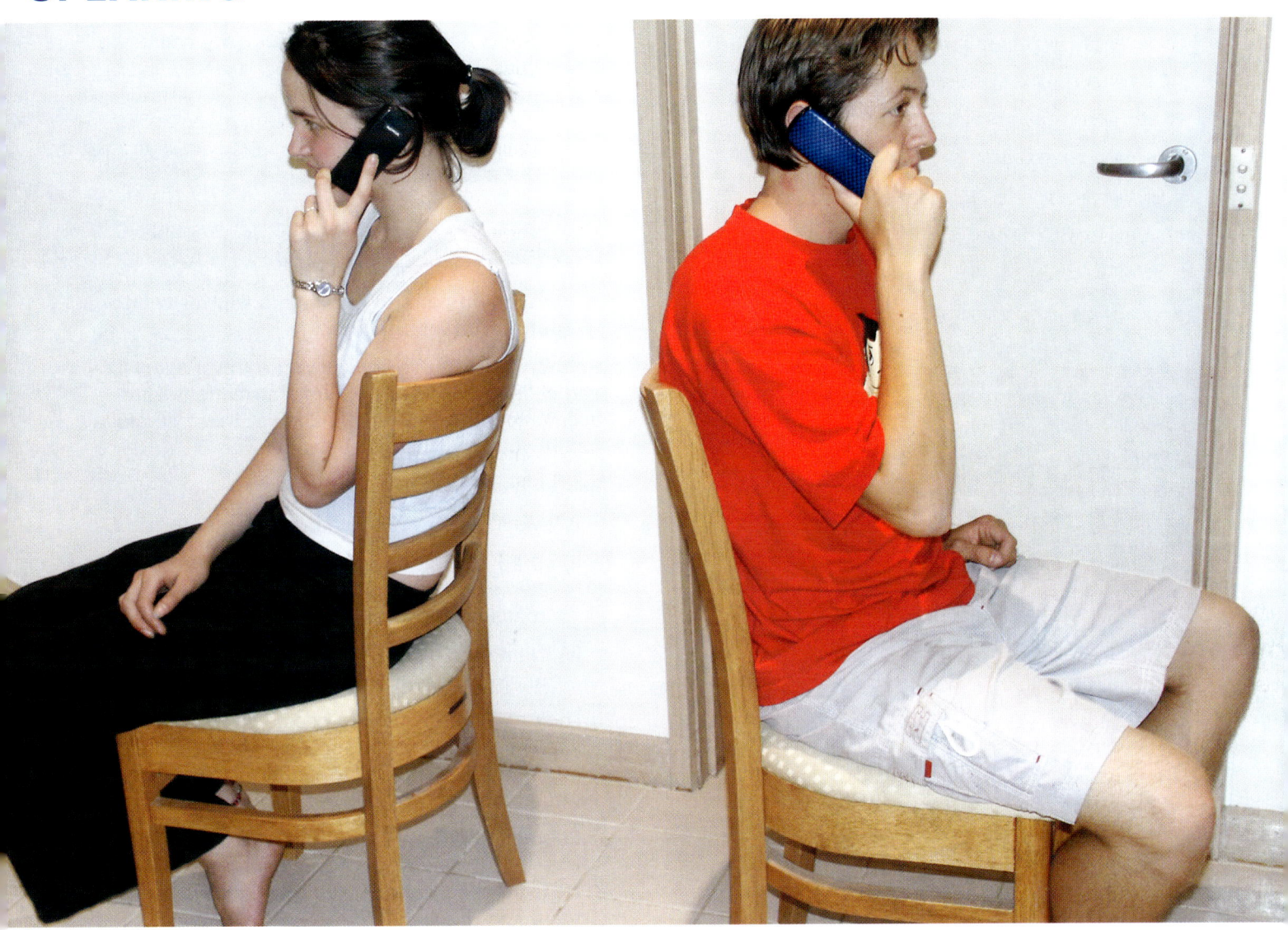

11. Tourist role-plays

In this role-play there are the three places you can go to for a holiday: Kaikoura, Wellington and the South Island. The role-play involves you and your partner playing a different role for the location you choose.

Find a partner and decide which of the places you would like to visit: Kaikoura, Wellington or the South Island. For each location you will see there are two roles; one person has Card A and the other Card B. Each of these is a different person.

With your partner collect a role-play card from your teacher and decide who will be the person on Card A and who will be the person in Card B.

In the role-play you will act out the person described on your card. Read the card carefully and think about what you would say to the other person.

a. Work together to decide what questions need to be asked and what answers should be given. You may wish to write them down. Practise asking the questions and giving the answers to each other. Then, start the role-play. Sit with your back to your partner and go through the conversations. Remember to sound and act like that person you are pretending to be. Swap roles and go through the conversation again. Decide who sounds best in each role and practise a few times.

b. When you feel that you have a good act, with the questions and the answers all following each other smoothly, act out your role-play in front of the class.

APPLICATION

12. Work in pairs to organise a trip for two to Rotorua for one week.

Before you start this activity visit a travel agent and collect brochures on tourist attractions and accommodation in Rotorua. Look at these carefully before you start the questions below.

a. On a blank map of NZ:

   i) Mark where you live and mark in Rotorua.

   ii) Draw the route you would take to get to Rotorua. Remember you can only travel where there are roads or a ferry service, unless you plan to fly.

   iii) Name the places you will go through on the way and mark them on your map.

b. Look at the brochures to decide where you will stay. Assume you will spend three nights in Rotorua. Write an email you can send to the accommodation centre where you want to book accommodation in Rotorua.

c. Send another email to the travel company to say that you wish to stay in the accommodation above, and that you need to book your travel arrangements to get there.

d. Look at the travel brochures on Rotorua to decide what you would like to see around Rotorua. Look at a map of Rotorua in one of the brochures to see where these places are. Explain to a partner why you decided to see a particular place.

e. So you can make sure of seeing everything you want to see you should write up a travel itinerary. This is a list with all the places you wish to visit in Rotorua and when you will see each place. The following table will help you do this. It also has a column where you can record whether you liked or disliked that activity.

Travel itinerary

Itinerary for ....

Trip destination: Rotorua

Date	Arrival time	Departure time	Tourist attra

Unit 4   Exploring New Zealand

REVISION

13. Using the information you have learned in this unit, answer these questions.

a. Is Rotorua near Taupo?

b. Is Auckland in the North Island?

c. Is Christchurch in the North Island?

d. Are there ski fields on the mountains in Queenstown?

e. What will you see in the water in the Bay of Islands?

f. Can you go skiing in Auckland?

g. Can you visit the Houses of Parliament in Wellington?

h. Is Christchurch the 'city of sails'?

i. Where will you see boiling mud?

14. Read the information about Auckland and answer the questions.

Auckland, the largest city in New Zealand, is the home to one third of New Zealand's population. It is the 'maritime playground' of New Zealand, as it has two magnificent harbours, Waitemata Harbour and Manukau Harbour.

Harbour cruises are available and you can catch a ferry to one of the nearby islands such as Waiheke Island and Great Barrier Island, or simply across the harbour to Devonport.

You can see magnificent views from Rangitoto Island which was formed from a volcano only 600 years ago.

There is a large variety of shops and restaurants in Auckland, and the Auckland Museum is known for its wonderful masterpieces of Maori art and displays of New Zealand's natural history and birdlife.

a. Name two islands which are close to Auckland.

b. What island is only 600 years old?

c. How can you travel to Devonport?

d. What can you see at the Auckland Museum?

e. Describe a 'maritime playground' in your own words.

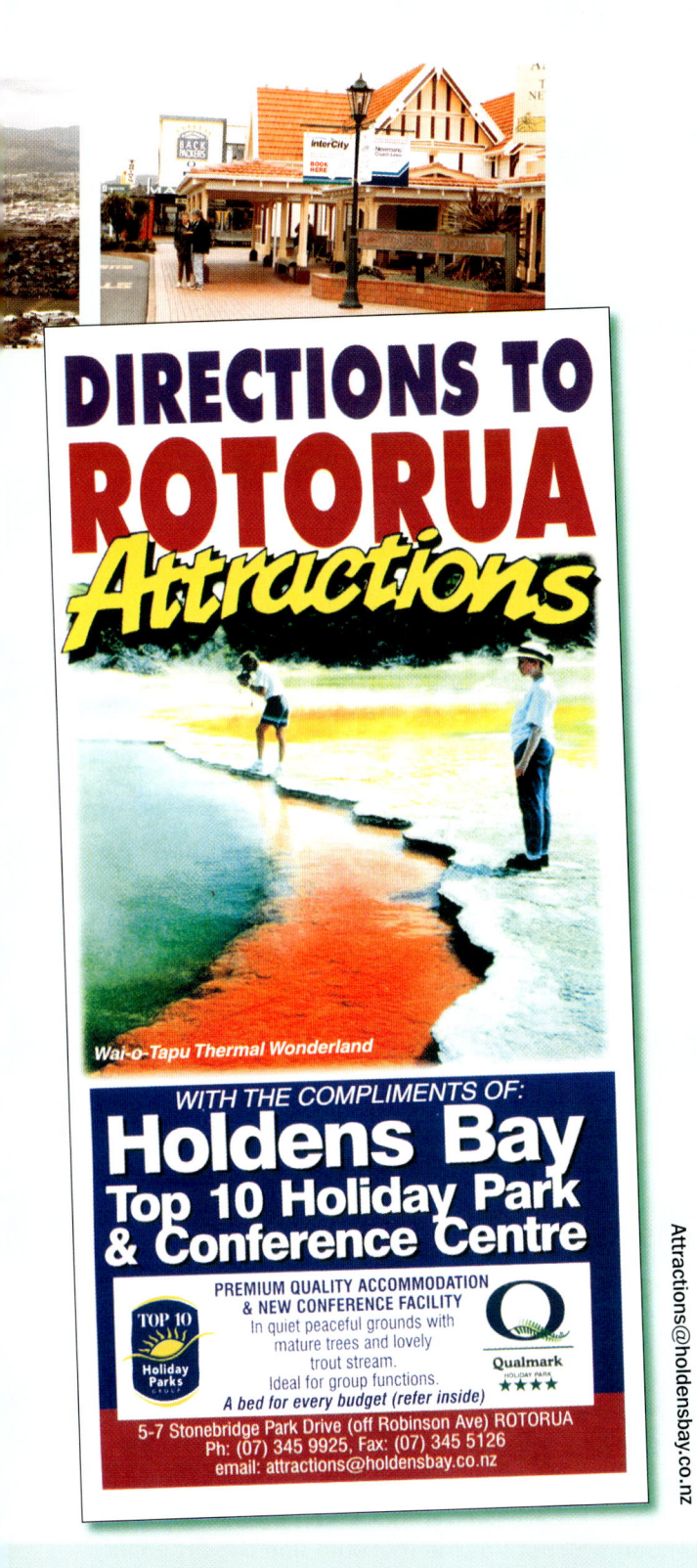

mmodation	Location	Activity	Like/dislike

41

15. Read the information about Christchurch and answer the questions.

Christchurch, situated in Canterbury, is the largest city in the South Island and has a population of over 320,000. It is famous for its beautiful parks and gardens and is called New Zealand's 'garden city'. The population is cosmopolitan and, in addition to scenic attractions and adventure tourism attractions, Christchurch has a variety of nightclubs, bars, theatres and a casino for people who enjoy going out in the evenings.

Christchurch also has many old buildings housing museums, craft and art galleries, and which are well worth a visit.

a. What is the meaning of cosmopolitan?
b. What is the population of Christchurch?
c. Where is Christchurch?
d. What can you do in the evening in Christchurch?
e. What is Christchurch famous for?

16. From the activities below write sentences that are true for you saying what you can/can't do and what you like/dislike.

Example: skiing *I like skiing.*

a. bungy jumping _____
b. horseriding _____
c. bushwalks _____
d. swimming with dolphins _____
e. sailing _____
f. jet-boat rides _____
g. white-water rafting _____
h. kayaking _____
i. windsurfing _____

17. Write an email to a backpacker hostel, booking accommodation for six people for three nights. Include the following:

a. What type of room you want.
b. Ask how you get to the city centre from the hostel and how long it would take.
c. Ask whether you can cook your own meals in the rooms.
d. Include the dates you are going to need accommodation.
e. State how many people require accommodation.

GRAMMAR

Can

'Can' has three main uses: ability, possibility and permission.

A positive statement takes the form: *I can ski. It can be very cold in Queenstown. You can use your credit card.*

A negative statement takes the form: *I can't ski. I can't ski if there isn't any snow. You can't use your credit card.*

A question takes the form: *Can you ski? Can you come with me?*

Like

A person's preference is expressed using the verb 'like'. For example: *I like skiing, I don't like swimming.*

When asking a question the auxiliary verb 'do' is used. For example: *Do you like skiing? Don't you like swimming?*

VOCABULARY

skiing / bungy jumping / sailing / white-water rafting / kayak / bushwalk / backpacker hostel / whale / dolphin / receptionist / parliament / museum / art gallery / geothermal / volcano / lake

TAPESCRIPTS

Tapescript 1a

We went to Auckland for the holidays. It's a big city for New Zealand – the biggest, and there was lots to do. It was a real change from living in Ashburton. We went for a sail on the Americas' Cup yacht NZL40 and it was great! You can work as a crew member or just sit and watch other people work – I watched!

We also went to the underwater aquarium – it was awesome – I really liked it, but I didn't really enjoy the afternoon we spent at the museum and the art gallery.

Tapescript 1b

We've just got back from the October holidays – we went skiing in Queenstown. Although the sun was shining, it was still quite cold, and there was plenty of snow. I can't ski very well but my friends can, and we all had a wonderful time!

The scenery in Queenstown is beautiful, the mountains look fantastic when they are covered with snow and you can almost see right through the water in Lake Wakatipu, because it is so clean!

We went to do a bungy jump, but only one of us actually did one. She said it was absolutely awesome, but most of us were just happy to watch!

Tapescript 1c

My friends and I went to Rotorua for a long weekend – it's quite different from anywhere else I've been. You can see steam rising from the ground, even in the middle of the city, and there are lots of places you can visit to see boiling mud and boiling water rising into the air – I think they're called geysers!

We went to a Maori concert party and hangi on the Saturday night. The concert was wonderful but I didn't really like the hangi food.

It was a really interesting weekend, but it takes a long time to get used to the smell!

Tapescript 2

Receptionist (R) Hello, this is NZ Tourist Information Centre. Can I help you?

Student (St) Good morning. I'd like to book a seven-day holiday in the South Island. I don't have much money but I want to see as much as possible. I will need accommodation and transport.

R You have several options, but the cheapest way to do this would be to join a bus tour and stay at youth or backpacker hostels. It would also be cheaper if you did not have to do this in the school holidays.

St Sorry, but I have no choice. I'll have to do it in the holidays. I'm a student here and the holidays are the only free time I have. How much is the cheapest tour?

R We have a five-day South Island Explorer Package which goes around the South Island, staying at places of interest. These include Kaikoura, Christchurch, Queenstown, Dunedin and Fox Glacier. If you stay at the hostels in shared rooms this can be as cheap as $75/day.

St Does this include food?

R It includes breakfast and dinner but you would have to buy your lunches and any other snacks you want.

St That sounds good. Are there usually young people on those tours? I don't want to go on a trip with a lot of people older than me.

R Yes, that type of tour is designed for young people.

St What days of the week does it leave?

R Those trips leave Picton on Sundays, Tuesdays and Thursdays each week.

St My holidays start next Friday. Is there a trip I could join on Sunday?

R Ooh, you've left it very late. Let me check. No sorry, Sunday and Tuesday are full, but there are two spaces left on Thursday.

St OK. Do I have to get myself to Picton?

R Yes. Where are you now?

St Wellington.

R OK. Do you want me to book you on the ferry? There's one that leaves at 01:30 which would get you to Picton at 04:30. As the tour bus leaves from the ferry terminal at 8 am, that would be perfect for you.

St How much will it cost?

R How old are you?

St Sixteen.

R The ferry will be $40 each way and the trip $375 making a total of $455.

St That's great! My parents said I could spend $500 on a holiday. Can I please do the booking now?

R Certainly. I will need to get some details from you …

Unit 5 — Healthy Food or Fast Food?

Grammar: Countable and uncountable nouns: *a pie/some rice*. Some and any: *Can I have some eggs? There aren't any left.* How many: *a few/a lot/a little/not much/some.*

Vocabulary: Food and drink.

STARTER

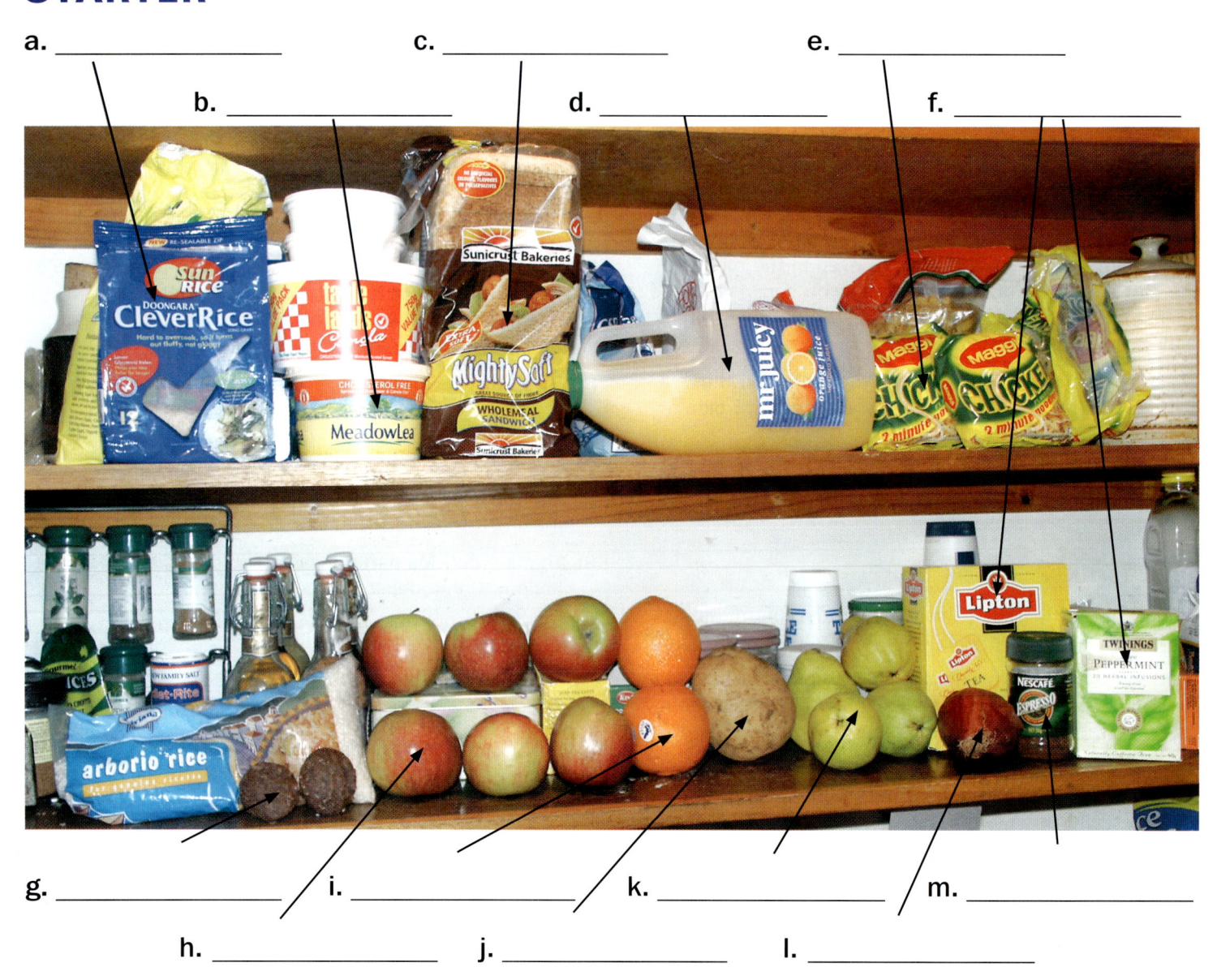

a. _____
b. _____
c. _____
d. _____
e. _____
f. _____
g. _____
h. _____
i. _____
j. _____
k. _____
l. _____
m. _____

1. Name the food items on the pantry shelves. Put *a*, *an* or *some* in front of each noun.

Example: *some oranges, an egg.*

2. Draw a similar chart and ask other students in the room to tell you if they like or dislike particular foods and fill in the chart.

Write some sentences about what you find out. For example: *Three people like eggs but six people don't.*

Foods People Like and Dislike

	Likes	Dislikes
noodles	10	2
eggs	3	6
potato	5	6

Unit 5   Healthy Food or Fast Food?

3. You have decided to eat healthier food and get fit this year.

Divide your page into three and enter the foods in the box into one of three categories: foods to eat a lot of, foods to eat in moderation, foods to eat very little of.

> pies eggs rice potatoes apples oranges
> lettuce chocolate tomatoes bread
> noodles meat butter ice-cream cheese
> cabbage cauliflower carrots cake biscuits
> chips milk cream cola wine soft drink
> juice nuts beer

Foods for healthy eating

Foods to eat a lot of	
Foods to eat in moderation	
Foods to eat very little of	

4. Using the list of food items in activity 3, ask a partner questions about the foods.

Example: *Do you like noodles? Yes I do.*

5. Fill in the gaps with *a, an, some, any, much, many*.

Refer to the Grammar section on countable and uncountable nouns.

a. Would you like _____ tea?

Yes, I'd love _____ cup, with milk and sugar please.

b. Are there _____ eggs in the fridge?

There are _____, but not many.

c. Is there _____ milk in that box?

No, there isn't _____ left.

d. How _____ sugar is there in the bowl?

Not _____, shall I get _____ more?

e. Have we got _____ biscuits?

Yes, they are _____ in the tin.

6. Look at the picture of the table and list everything you can see on it.

For example: *some bread, some cucumber.*

45

7. Write out the sentences using the correct phrases.

a. *How much/how many* apples are there?

_____

b. *How much/how many* milk is left in the glass?

_____

c. *How much/how many* rice do we have in the pantry?

_____

d. *How much/how many* students are there in this class?

_____

e. *How much/how many* margarine have we got?

_____

LISTENING

8. Listen to the conversation on Tapescript 1 and fill in the gaps.

M Hi Tony, are you getting _____ from the canteen?

T Yes. I'm just on my way. What _____ you getting?

M I don't know. I should be good and get a salad ____ _____ and some fruit, but it's so cold and I love the _____ at the canteen.

T I'm getting _____ pie and chips, and probably _____ caramel square and _____ soft drink as well. I don't know why you try to be good, just eat what you like!

M That's alright for you. You don't seem to put on weight and boys don't seem to care about those things anyway!

T I guess I'm lucky, but I do play _____ of sport to keep fit.

M Mmm! Look at the queue at the chip counter! I think there may be _____ good things about eating healthy food – you don't have to wait so long to get it!

T Yeah! You might be right! See you later!

M OK. _____!

9. Have you heard of Charles Dickens and the story of Oliver Twist?

Discuss life in England 200 years ago with your teacher – in particular what happened to people if they were very poor.

Listen to the song *Food, Glorious Food.* (Glorious means wonderful, very nice.)

a. What do you think the singer's life is like? Do you think he gets enough to eat?

b. List the foods mentioned in the song. (Check with Transcript 2.)

_____
_____
_____
_____
_____
_____

READING

Discovering the world of pies

Comedian Jon Bridges takes us on a journey around the country in celebration of New Zealand's most popular and **traditional** fare in Who Ate All the Pies? (DNZ, tonight at 8.30pm on TV One).

And with not a pork pie in sight Jon travels from Auckland to Invercargill in a hot yellow mini in **pursuit** of adventure. But this time the **exploits** are about visiting pie-carts and **patisseries** gathering secrets from master bakers and discovering why New Zealanders eat more pies than any other country (except Australia).

In fact every year New Zealand polishes off 123 million pies a year.

And director Michael Huddleston says in the two weeks of making Who Ate All the Pies? the crew ate more than 30 of the tasty snacks.

"My personal favourite was a mutton pie, which was made in Palmerston in the South Island from a **traditional** Scottish recipe," says Huddleston. "While Jon **preferred** a Big Ben or a potato top."

"After making the **documentary** I'll only eat a good pie now … and a good pie is one with **soul**," he reveals.

Huddleston is the first to admit that during filming they hardly came across a bad pie. During their travels Jon tussles with the metal **detector** at Ponsonby Pies, gets the **low-down** on the demise of the Georgie Pie chain, and meets a lone travelling salesman who eats over 700 pies a year.

"We do talk to the Heart Foundation about the effects on your health of eating pies. The Foundation advises eating one pie a month but for the purposes of this **documentary** we had to ignore it."

During their travels Jon meets the Tiger Woods of pies – baker James Buckrell, who has won a total of nine gold medals at the NZ Pie Awards – seven more than his nearest competitor.

Jon also stops in Matamata and meets Hangi in a Pie **visionary** Ron Smith before setting off for Wellington where he **consults** a pie historian and finds out some very interesting facts, including the first pie was probably created in Greece.

Then down to the Mainland Jon is introduced to the ex-cop who **founded** Quentins, and travels to the home of legendary Jimmy Pies – the mighty town of Roxburgh – where he learns that the best pie ever seen in New Zealand **contained**, wait for it, green apple.

"This is an **affectionate** look at our humble Kiwi fare,"

says Huddleston. "And it's also a **celebration** of why New Zealanders love it so much."

Jon shows his **admiration** by **composing** poems about different pies along the way, and also enters the New Zealand Pie Awards with his own creation.

To find out how he goes, and to treat yourself to one of the country's favourite food, watch Who Ate All the Pies?

from Rotorua Daily Post

10. Skim this newspaper article which appeared in the Rotorua Daily Post to get the general meaning of the article. Then work with a partner and use your dictionaries to find the meanings of the words in the box.

Once you have checked the meaning is correct with your teacher, add the word and meaning to your vocabulary notebook. Highlight any other words you do not understand and add them to the list.

> patisserie traditional low-down visionary
>
> legendary affectionate pursuit exploits
>
> preferred documentary detector soul
>
> consults founded contained celebration
>
> admiration composing

11. Once you have understood the meaning of any words you do not know reread the article taken from the Rotorua Daily Post and answer the following questions.

This approach of skimming an article, checking unknown words and then rereading can be used for all unfamiliar reading. Find other newspaper articles and try to read and understand what it is saying by using this approach.

a. What country eats more pies than New Zealand?

b. How many pies are eaten in New Zealand each year?

c. According to the Heart Foundation, how often should people eat pies?

d. What do you think the writer means when he talks about 'the Tiger Woods of pies'?

e. What fillings might there be in 'a hangi in a pie'?

f. What filling was in 'the best pie ever seen in New Zealand'?

g. What part of New Zealand is referred to as 'the Mainland'?

WRITING

12. Look at the food pyramid and discuss what foods fit into each category with your teacher.

Why do you think the food pyramid has been developed?

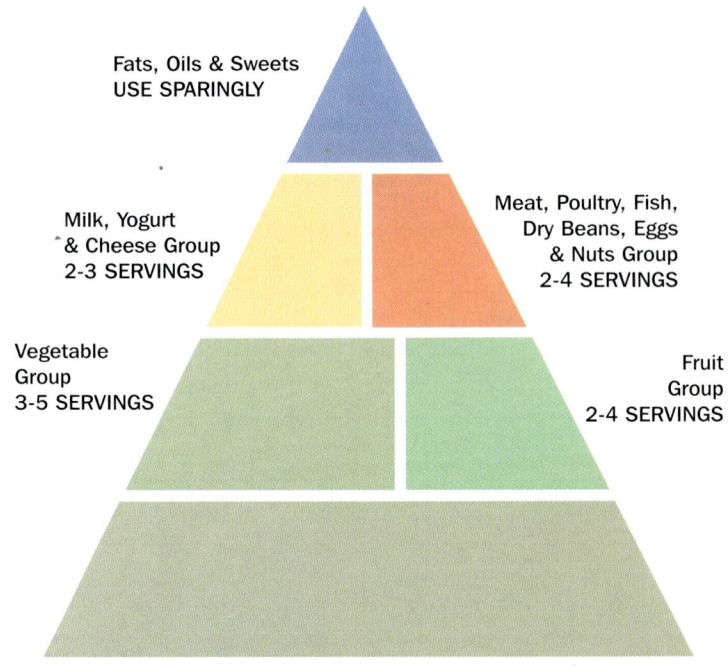

Fats, Oils & Sweets
USE SPARINGLY

Milk, Yogurt & Cheese Group
2-3 SERVINGS

Meat, Poultry, Fish, Dry Beans, Eggs & Nuts Group
2-4 SERVINGS

Vegetable Group
3-5 SERVINGS

Fruit Group
2-4 SERVINGS

Bread, Cereal, Rice & Pasta Group
3-5 SERVINGS

13. Write out what you have eaten in the last 24 hours, putting the foods into the right categories on the food pyramid.

Foods eaten in the last 24 hours

fats and sugar	
dairy products	
fruit & vegetables	
red meats	
poultry & fish	
bread & cereals	

14. You have been given the task of planning the meals for the next two days for a homestay family, of two adults and two children about your age, and yourself.

Think about the ages of the people you are feeding and take into account people's likes and dislikes. Refer to the food pyramid and work in groups of three. Share your ideas with the class.

a. Write down what you would have for breakfast, lunch, dinner and snacks.

b. Write a shopping list for the two days. Say how much of each item you would buy.

c. Look at your group's shopping list and menu with another group and comment on how healthy and practical your group's plans are.

Menu

	Breakfast	Lunch	Dinner
Day 1			
Day 2			

Shopping list

Day	Meal	Items to buy	Quantity
1	Breakfast		
	Lunch		
	Dinner		
	Other snacks		
2	Breakfast		
	Lunch		
	Dinner		
	Other snacks		

SPEAKING

15. Ask your teacher to arrange for you to visit the canteen (or a local dairy if you do not have a canteen) when the staff are not busy.

Write out five questions to ask the staff. For example: *What do you buy? Why do you buy it? Do you consider price, health value, student demand?* Write up a list of all the food that is available from your school canteen.

16. Survey the members of your class and find out what people commonly buy at the canteen or local dairy, and what other foods they would like to be able to buy.

Food buying habits

What do you buy at	Person 1	Person 2
School Canteen		
Local Dairy		

17. Present the information to the class.

Identify the foods people can buy now, what foods they would like to buy, and whether they want healthier food and why?

18. Class debate. Working in groups of three students prepare a debate arguing one side of the following question: The canteen should sell healthier foods even if it is more expensive.

With the class teacher organise a class debate. (If you do not have a canteen you could debate: Fast foods shops should sell healthier food.)

APPLICATION

19. You have been given the task of working with a group of students to develop a new range of food for your school canteen.

a. Use the surveys about food preferences from earlier in this unit, plus the healthy food pyramid, to make a list of foods you think should be available in your canteen.

b. Look at each of the photos of food and identify which should be in your canteen by placing a tick in the space. If you do not think that food should be there place a cross in the box. Explain to your group why you have placed a tick or a cross against each food.

Unit 5   Healthy Food or Fast Food?

20. Design a full-page advertising poster for the new foods you are introducing. Have a picture of the new food and write reasons why people should buy it.

REVISION

23. Name each item putting *a*, *an*, or *some* in front of each noun.

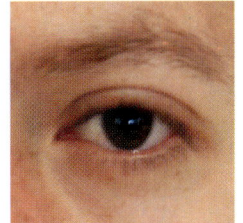

a. _____   b. _____   c. _____

d. _____   e. _____   f. _____

g. _____   h. _____   i. _____

j. _____   k. _____   l. _____

m. _____   n. _____   o. _____

Cheap! Hot! Nutritious! Multi flavours!

21. Find a partner and write up a dialogue for the following situation at the canteen.

- a student can't make up their mind what to have for lunch
- a canteen assistant helps the student make his/her choice
- the student politely requests the food he/she has decided on.

Once you have completed your dialogue read it out with a different student playing each part.

22. You have decided to make your lunch and take it to school each day and your homestay parents have told you to give them a list of things you would like them to buy.

Make a list of the food you would need. For example: *some bread, some fruit*.

24. Use the blank food pyramid and place the items of food from the following list onto the pyramid in the correct place.

a. cheese
b. tomatoes
c. chicken legs
d. fish
e. hazelnut spread
f. pasta
g. yoghurt
h. lollies/sweets
i. eggs
j. apples

Food Pyramid

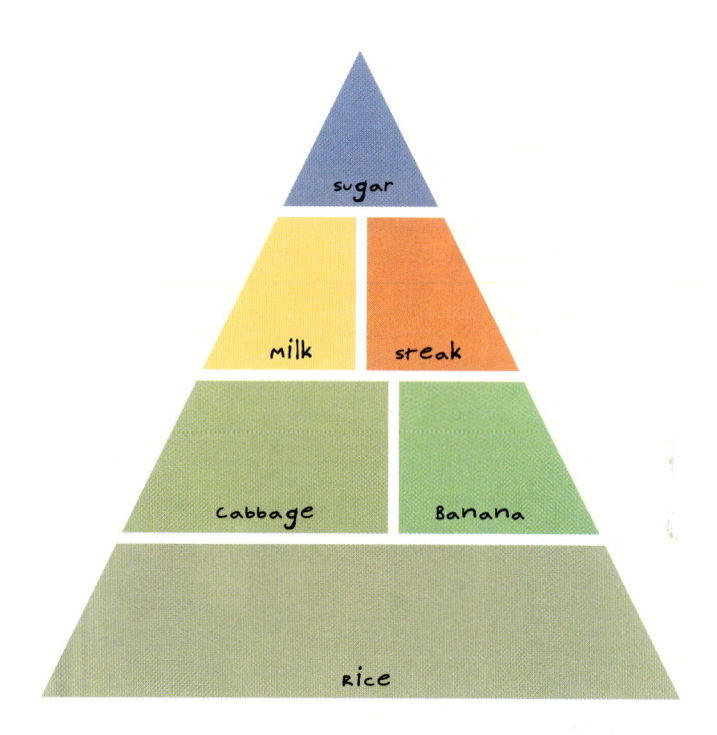

(pyramid labelled: sugar / milk / steak / cabbage / Banana / rice)

GRAMMAR

Countable and uncountable nouns

Countable nouns can be both singular and plural. For example: *the egg/the eggs, an apple/some apples, that boy/those boys*. Countable nouns can follow *a* and *an*, *the*, *a number*, *this*, *those*, *some*, *many* and *that*.

Uncountable nouns have no plural. They refer to things that you cannot count. For example: *bread/coffee/rice*. Uncountable nouns do not follow *a* or *an*, but they can follow *some*, *much*, *a little*, *the*.

Many is used with countable nouns, *much* with uncountable nouns, *a lot* can be used with countable and uncountable nouns. For example: *How many eggs?/not many eggs/a lot of eggs/How much juice?/not much juice/a lot of juice*.

Some and any

Some replaces *a* and *an* when we are talking about more than one countable noun, or about an uncountable noun. *Some* is used only in positive statements. *Any* replaces *some* in questions and negatives. For example: *I want some apples from the shop. Do you want any apples from the shop? I don't want any apples from the shop.*

VOCABULARY

healthy / unhealthy / cakes / pies / sandwiches / carrots / cauliflower / cabbage / meat / caramel square / fillings / weight (put on weight) / hangi / pyramid / salad-filled roll / nutrition (nutritious) / biscuits / snacks /

TAPESCRIPTS

Tapescript 1

M Hi Tony, are you getting lunch from the canteen?

T Yes, I'm on my way. What are you getting?

M I don't know. I should be good and get a salad sandwich and some fruit. But it's so cold and I love the chips at the canteen.

T I'm getting a pie and chips, and probably a caramel square and a soft drink as well. I don't know why you try to be good, just eat what you like!

M That's alright for you. You don't seem to put on weight and boys don't seem to care about those things anyway!

T I guess I'm lucky, but I do play lots of sport to keep fit.

M Mmm! Look at the queue at the chip counter! I think there may be some good things about eating healthy food – you don't have to wait so long to get it!

T Yeah! You might be right! See you later!

M OK. Bye!

Tapescript 2

FOOD, GLORIOUS FOOD

from Oliver

Is it worth the waiting for?
If we live 'til eighty-four
All we ever get is gru...el!
Ev'ry day we say our prayer –
Will they change the bill of fare?
Still we get the same old gru...el!
There is not a crust, not a crumb can we find,
Can we beg, can we borrow, or cadge,
But there's nothing to stop us from getting a thrill
When we all close our eyes and ima...gine

Food, glorious food!
Hot sausage and mustard!
While we're in the mood –
Cold jelly and custard!
Pease pudding and saveloys!
What next is the question?
Rich gentlemen have it, boys,
In-di-gestion!

Food, glorious food!
We're anxious to try it.
Three banquets a day –
Our favourite diet!
Just picture a great big steak –
Fried, roasted or stewed.
Oh, food, wonderful food,
Marvellous food, glorious food.

Food, glorious food!
What is there more handsome?
Gulped, swallowed or chewed –
Still worth a king's ransom.
What is it we dream about?
What brings on a sigh?
Piled peaches and cream , about
Six feet high!

Food, glorious food!
Eat right through the menu.
Just loosen your belt
Two inches and then you
Work up a new appetite.
In this interlude –
Then food, once again, food,
Fabulous food, glorious food.

Food, glorious food!
Don't care what it looks like –
Burned! Underdone! Crude!
Don't care what the cook's like.
Just thinking of growing fat –
Our senses go reeling
One moment of knowing that
Full-up feeling!

Food, glorious food!
What wouldn't we give for
That extra bit more –
That's all that we live for
Why should we be fated to
Do nothing but brood
On food, magical food,
Wonderful food, marvellous food, fabulous food,
Beautiful food, glorious food.

How Much Do You Remember?

Units 1–5

1. Put the words in the list in alphabetical order. Then tick which group they belong to. Some words may be in two groups.

	Food	Transport	Sport	Places	Activities	People
school						
bike						
car						
man						
woman						
sport						
lunch						
husband						
wife						
brother						
sister						
name						
country						
shop						
canteen						
holiday						
sailing						
bungy						
kayak						
chocolate						

/10

2. Write the verb in the brackets in the correct form.

a. My brother _____ (go) to school in Korea.
b. We _____ (go) to school in New Zealand.
c. The teacher _____ (come) to school by car.
d. I _____ (play) basketball on Wednesdays.
e. He _____ (play) rugby on Saturday.

/5

3. Fill in the details on the form below for yourself.

First name: _____
Surname: _____
Nationality: _____
Age: _____
School: _____

/5

4. Read the paragraph below and answer the questions.

Yoshi and Mariko have been married for ten years. They lived with Yoshi's parents Keiko and Yuchi for the first two years of their marriage and then moved into an apartment of their own. They have two children: a girl named Sue and a boy named Hiroaki. Sue is five years old and Hiroaki is two.

a. Who is Yoshi's father? _____
b. Who is Mariko's husband? _____
c. Who is Yoshi's daughter? _____
d. Who is Mariko's son? _____
e. Who is Sue's brother? _____

/5

5. Circle the word in each group that doesn't fit and explain why.

a. envelope   stamp   radio   mailbox
_____

b. doctor   prescription   medicine   teller
_____

c. credit   emergency   deposit   withdrawal
_____

d. walk   left   inside   right
_____

e. tickets   school   travel agent   holiday
_____

/5

How Much Do You Remember? Units 1–5

6. Where would you go if you had the following problems?

a. You feel unwell.
_____

b. You need to post a letter.
_____

c. You need new glasses.
_____

d. You want to put your money somewhere safe.
_____

e. You need to register your car.
_____

/5

7. Write the name of each part of the body in the space provided.

mouth	stomach	back
hair	fingers	nose
neck	hips	head
chin	legs	eye
shoulders	feet	ear
arms	hands	elbow
chest	toes	knee

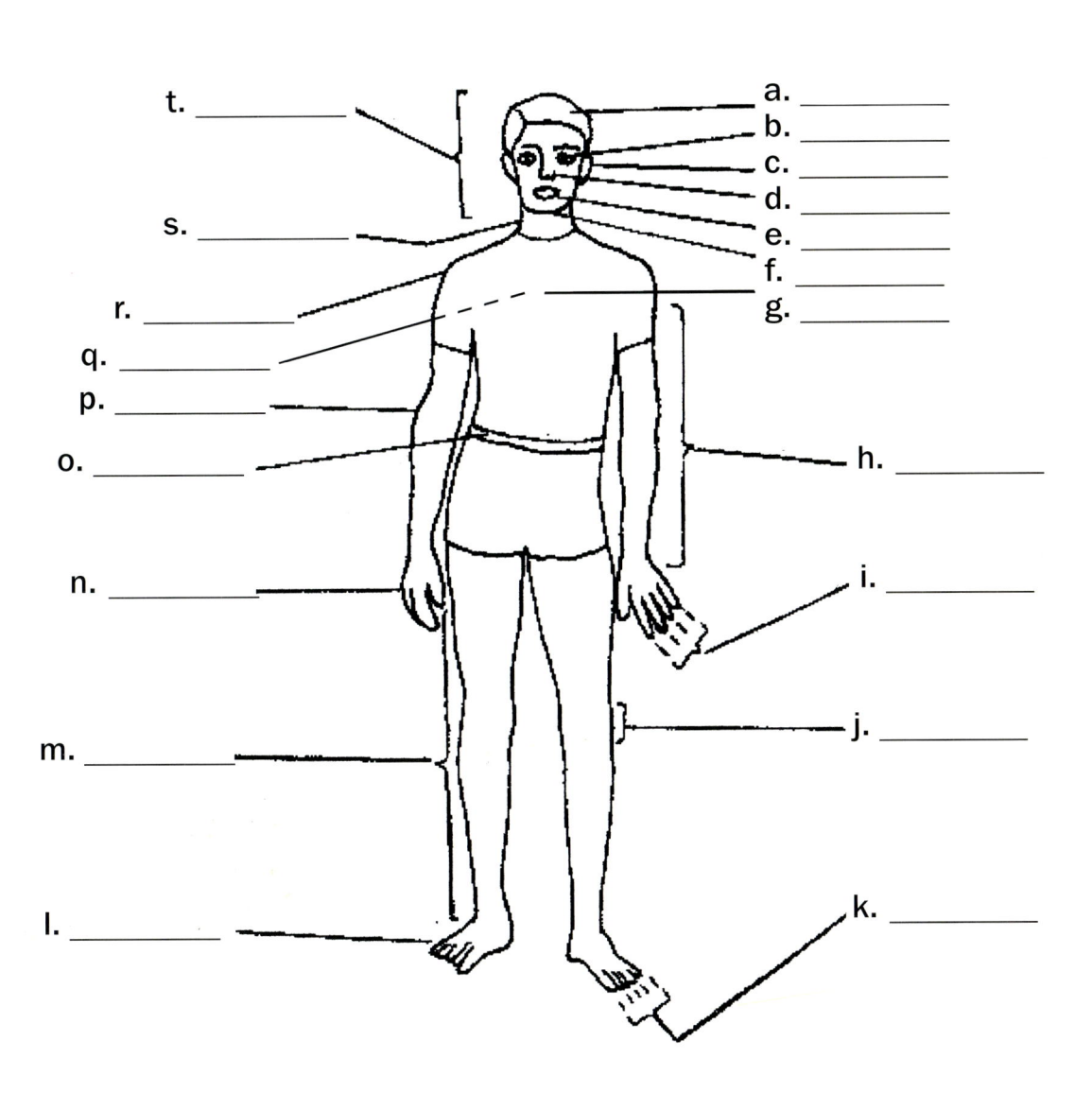

/15

t. _____
s. _____
r. _____
q. _____
p. _____
o. _____
n. _____
m. _____
l. _____

a. _____
b. _____
c. _____
d. _____
e. _____
f. _____
g. _____
h. _____
i. _____
j. _____
k. _____

55

English Zone Elementary Student Book

8. Write advice for the following situations.

a. You have fallen over and cut your knee.
   You should _____

b. You have a cold.
   _____

c. You have an exam tomorrow.
   _____

d. You can't see clearly when you drive.
   _____

e. The lady has broken her tooth.
   _____

/5

9. Match the verb with its body part.

kick	eyes
talk	teeth
write	foot
bite	hand
see	mouth

/5

10. Write the name of each object in the space provided.

a. _____ b. _____

c. _____ d. _____

e. _____ f. _____

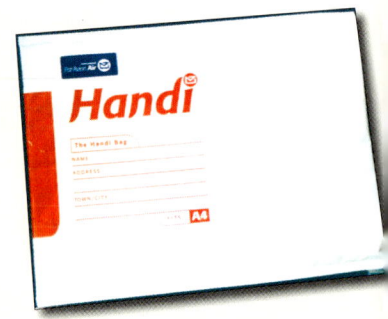

g. _____ h. _____

i. _____ j. _____

/5

56

How Much Do You Remember? Units 1-5

11. Write the names for the following things (half mark for the correct word and half mark for spelling it correctly).

a. You put a letter in this.
   e_____

b. You take a prescription here to get medicine.
   c_____

c. You use this to get money out of a machine.
   c_____ c_____

d. You go to this person to get new glasses.
   o_____

e. You use these to see with.
   e_____

f. Your mouth, nose and eyes are on this.
   f_____

g. Your doctor looks at this when he/she wants to see inside your body.
   X_____

h. This part of your body hurts if you have food poisoning.
   s_____

i. You have five of these on each hand.
   f_____

j. If your head hurts, you have one of these.
   h_____

/10

12. Fill in the gaps with a preposition from the box that makes the sentence correct. You may use a preposition more than once.

| on | in | near | in | at |

a. Christchurch is a city _____ the South Island of New Zealand.

b. You can go skiing _____ the Remarkables _____ Queenstown.

c. Taupo is _____ Rotorua.

d. She is a receptionist _____ a backpacker hotel.

/5

13. Name the five places described below.

a. Known for its boiling mud   R_____
b. New Zealand's 'garden city' C_____
c. Where was the Americas' Cup held A_____
d. Where the Treaty of Waitangi was signed
   B_____ of I_____

/5

14. Make words out of these letters. All the words have been in Units 1–5 of this book.

Example: toba boat

a. yakak   _____
b. mseumu   _____
c. ovloanc   _____
d. npoldhi   _____
e. lisanig   _____
f. yungb umpjngi   _____ _____
g. quruaima   _____
h. klae   _____
i. aftrnig   _____
j. cyaht   _____

/5

15. Put *a*, *an*, or *some* next to the items below.

a. _____ apple
b. _____ milk
c. _____ orange
d. _____ oranges
e. _____ banana
f. _____ cake
g. _____ piece of cake
h. _____ noodles
i. _____ bread
j. _____ lettuce

/5

16. Put *much*, *many*, *any* or *some* in the gaps below.

a. How _____ bananas are in the bowl?
b. How _____ milk is in the bottle?
c. There are not _____ eggs left.
d. There is not _____ margarine in the container.
e. Do you have _____ money?
f. No, but I have _____ credit left on my credit card.
g. How _____ boys are there in this class?
h. There are not _____ girls.
i. But, there are _____ adult students.
j. Will there be _____ time to watch a video?

/5

TOTAL   /100

Unit 6 — Good, Better, Best

Grammar: Comparative and superlative adjectives: *big/bigger/biggest, good/better/best, beautiful/more beautiful/most beautiful.*

Vocabulary: Descriptive adjectives: *expensive/famous/modern.*

STARTER

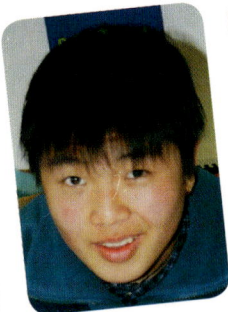

Name: Jong Kim
Age: 17 years
Height: 158 cm
Weight: 70 kg
Family: parents, one sister

Name: James Wei
Age: 14 years
Height: 140cm
Weight: 59 kg
Family: parents, no brothers or sisters

Name: Mariko Ito
Age: 16 years
Height: 135cm
Weight: 50 kg
Family: parents, one brother

1. Read the information about the students on the ID cards and then say whether the statements below are true or false.

Example: Jong is older than James.   *true*

a. James is taller than Jong.   _____
b. Jong is lighter than James.   _____
c. James is heavier than Jong.   _____
d. There are more people in Jong's family than in James's family.   _____
e. Mariko is the youngest of the three.   _____
f. James is the tallest of the three students.   _____
g. James has the smallest family.   _____
h. Jong is the heaviest student.   _____
i. James is the oldest of the three students.   _____

2. Match each adjective in Group 1 with an adjective from Group 2 with the opposite meaning by drawing a line between them.

Group 1	Group 2
quick	expensive
big	untidy
friendly	slow
kind	hard
soft	small
tall	closed
new	mean
open	old
cheap	short
tidy	unfriendly

Unit 6   Good, Better, Best

3.
Read the information about the four countries and then write eight sentences comparing them.

Example: *China is bigger than Japan. Japan has the highest life expectancy.*

Country	Population	Area (sq.km)	Life expectancy (years)
China	1,261,000,000	9,596,965	70
Japan	126,182,077	377,743	80
New Zealand	3,662,265	268,930	77
Australia	19,387,000	7,692,030	78

a. _____

b. _____

c. _____

d. _____

e. _____

f. _____

g. _____

h. _____

4.
Fill the gaps in the sentences below using the comparative form of the adjectives.

a. New Zealand is _____ than Australia. (*small*)

b. Japan is _____ than New Zealand. (*busy*)

c. Life in China is _____ than life in New Zealand. (*fast*)

d. Public transport in Japan is _____ than in New Zealand. (*good*)

e. Shopping in New Zealand is _____ than shopping in Japan. (*cheap*)

5.
Write five sentences comparing the size, population, things to do, pollution, cleanliness and transport in your home city with the city or town you live in in New Zealand.

Example: *Wellington is quieter than Beijing.*

a. _____

b. _____

c. _____

d. _____

e. _____

6.
Write out the correct sentence for each pair.

a. Last week was more wet than this week.
   Last week was wetter than this week.

b. He's heavier than his sister.
   He's more heavy than his sister.

c. I'm the most clever student in this class.
   I'm the cleverest student in this class.

d. My assignment was the best in the class.
   My assignment was the bestest in the class.

e. He's the most short student in the class.
   He's the shortest student in the class.

English Zone Elementary Student Book

LISTENING

7. Listen to Tapescript 1 and, while you are listening, write down the size, population, and life expectancy for each country in a table.

	Australia	Indonesia	Thailand
Area			
Population			
Life Expectancy			

8. Answer the following questions using the information you have written down.

a. Which is the biggest country by area?
b. Which is the smallest country by area?
c. Does Australia have a higher life expectancy than Indonesia?
d. Does Thailand have a lower life expectancy than Indonesia?
e. Which country has the largest population?
f. Which country has the smallest population?

9. Fill in the gaps using comparative and superlative adjectives.

a. The population of Thailand is _____ than the population of Australia.
b. The population of Indonesia is _____ than the population of Thailand.
c. In Indonesia, the life expectancy is _____ than in Thailand.
d. Australia is the _____ country of the three by area.
e. Thailand is the _____ country of the three by area.

10. Carefully look at the graph below comparing the areas of the three countries. Draw a bar graph of the population and life expectancy figures for the three countries. Make sure your graph has a title and that both axes are labelled.

Area of Selected Countries

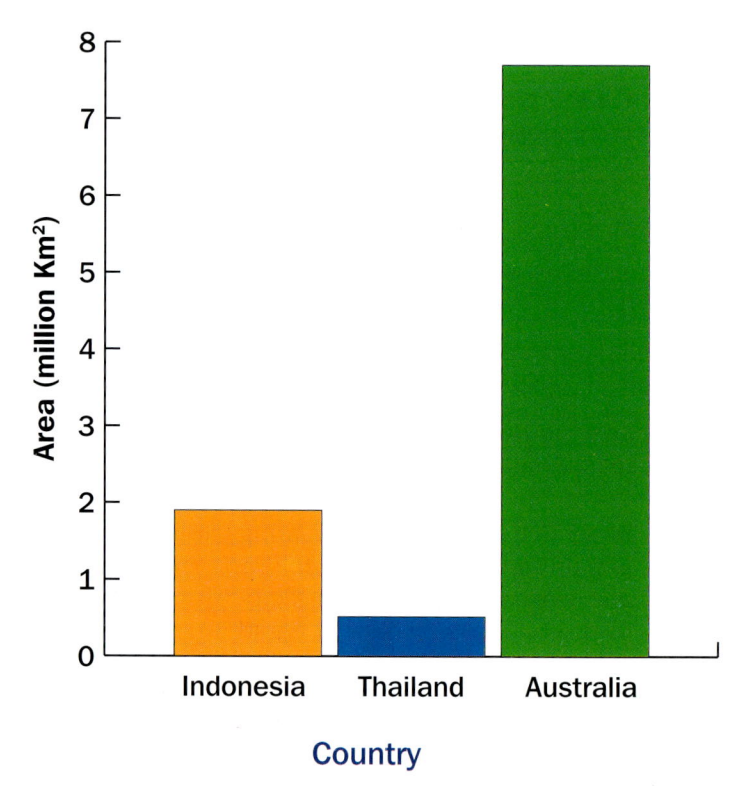

60

READING

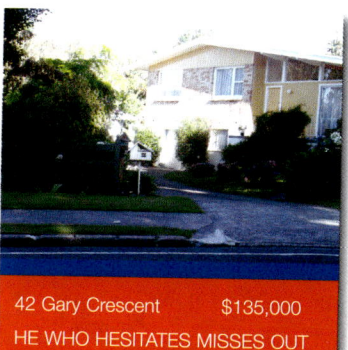

42 Gary Crescent $135,000
HE WHO HESITATES MISSES OUT
This weatherboard and brick 2 storey home has a comfortable style that will add pleasure to your life. Spacious and sunny, 4 bedrooms, 2 lounges, set on a flat section with lovely, mature, landscaped grounds. Be quick!
www.realestaterotorua.co.nz

5 HAPPY PLACE $234,000
A HOME DESIGNED FOR CHILDREN
No more sharing when you become the owner of this 5 bedroom nearly new home situated in a quiet court. Lovely indoor/outdoor flow to a very private garden.
www.realestaterotorua.co.nz

1025 OLD TAUTO ROAD $349,000
YOU'LL WELCOME WINTER!
You'll be very warm and cosy here where thermal heating is a great feature of this superb, private, 4 bedroom character home with mature gardens. Large living areas lead to sheltered gardens and it's all within walking distance to schools, shops and the golf course. At the end of a long day at the golf course, relax in your own thermally heated spa!
www.realestaterotorua.co.nz

11. Read the three advertisements for houses and answer the questions.

a. Which house has the most bedrooms?
b. Which house is cheapest?
c. Which house is most expensive?
d. Which house has the sheltered garden?
e. Which house do you think is the oldest? Why?

Prereading activity

Discuss fishing in New Zealand, types of fishing, equipment needed and who in the class has been fishing. If you haven't been fishing, talk to a partner about it, and what equipment you think you may need and why.

12. Read the newspaper article 'Smallest boat, shortest time, biggest fish', and answer the questions below.

Follow the procedure outlined in Unit 5 Activity 10: skim, identify words you don't understand, find their meaning, reread. Some of the words in this article which may prove difficult for you to understand have been printed in bold type. Add these words to your vocabulary notebook.

Smallest boat, shortest time, biggest fish

by Cherie Taylor in Rotorua

Paul King was in the smallest boat and out for the shortest time yet he brought in the biggest fish to be landed during the weekend's **Octobafest** fishing competition.

A broken wrist bone did not **hinder** the Fielding **sales representative** hooking a 5.5kg brown trout on Saturday evening.

'I could not believe it when I reeled it in and it was so big because it only took me about 30 minutes **to reel** it in about 5 metres,' he said.

On board a 30 year-old, four-metre ply-light **runabout**, Mr King hooked the fish using a traffic light lure in the shallow waters of Lake Rotorua's Sulphur Bay.

His **whopper** catch has won him a $150 rod and reel from Kilwell Sports for the biggest catch of the weekend.

He had made a **spur-of-the-moment** decision to take in a spot of fishing on his way home from dropping his partner at Auckland airport on her way to Canada.

Although Mr King has been fishing for about six years, this weekend's contest is the first he has entered.

'I just never thought of entering **previously** but I'm sure to want to enter a few more now,' he said.

Octobafest competition organiser Dave Scott, from the Lake Rotoiti Holiday Park, has been involved with fishing competitions since 1974. He said the trout Mr King caught was one of the biggest browns he had seen fished up around Rotorua lakes.

'We normally have lots of rainbow trout coming in because brown trout can be **wily old foxes** to hook,' he said.

The weekend's competition drew 32 entries.

from Rotorua Daily Post

a. How big was the smallest boat?
b. How big was the fish?
c. What was wrong with Paul King's arm?
d. What is another word for 'whopper'?
e. How long was the shortest time?

WRITING

13. Fill the gaps with the correct form of the adjective.

Example:

Life in New Zealand is *slower* than life in Japan. (*slow*)

Yes, larger populated countries have a much *faster* way of life. (*fast*)

a. My sister is much _____ than me. (*young*)

   Yes, you are a lot _____ . (*old*)

b. Electrical goods are _____ in New Zealand than in Hong Kong. (*expensive*)

   Yes, Hong Kong is _____ . (*cheap*)

c. I think the food in New Zealand is _____ than the food in Asia. (*bad*)

   Really? I think the food in New Zealand is _____ . (*good*)

d. The buildings in new cities are _____ than the buildings in older places. (*modern*)

   Yes, ancient cities have _____ buildings. (*old*)

14. Write a letter to someone in your home country comparing your last school at home, with your school in New Zealand.

Be sure to include the following points: size of school, number of students, subject difficulty, subject choices, strictness of teachers, sporting activities, and anything else you can think of. Use comparatives and superlatives when you can. Underline these when you use them. For example: *My New Zealand school is smaller than my school in China.*

---

29 June 2003

Dear Mum and Dad,

My school in New Zealand is much bigger than my school in Japan. You will not believe it. We have over 1,000 students in my school.

We also have a lot of new subjects we don't study at home. Everyone is interested in sport in New Zealand. They are very interested in rugby, but I have trouble understanding how it works, even though I try.

I have some great teachers, but they are not as strict as teachers are at home. Mr Newman is our maths teacher and he is really tough. He really demands that we work. And, I mean work hard. You are not allowed to talk in class. One student decided to eat his lunch in maths class. He was hungry as our lesson had not finished when the bell rang. Mr Newman was very angry! We almost missed lunch – all of us! Most teachers are very kind and help us to learn, even when it is hard for us to explain what is wrong. Often, I talk with other Japanese students when I do not understand things. They can help me learn. But if that does not work, I ask the teacher.

When I have time I will write to you about a lovely girl in my science class who comes from a town near our home.

Love

Yomiko

15. Answer the following questions about Yomiko's letter to home.

a. Where does Yomiko come from?

b. Are New Zealand students interested in sport?

c. Are teachers more or less strict in New Zealand than at home?

d. Should you eat in class in New Zealand?

e. If you have trouble understanding something in class, who should you ask for help?

f. Why might Yomiko ask her friends for help when she does not understand? What is good about this and why could it cause problems?

SPEAKING

> Boys are stronger than girls in all ways.

> No they're not, boys act like babies if they hurt themselves. Girls are much stronger.

16. Discuss the following statements with a partner. Do you agree or disagree with the statements and with each other? Circle your opinion below.

a. Boys are stronger than girls. agree/disagree

b. Girls are cleverer than boys. agree/disagree

c. Women are better drivers than men. agree/disagree

17. Make up questions using comparative or superlative forms of the adjective and the following words. Then ask three people each question.

Example: good/film/on

What is the best film on at the moment?

a. good/musical group/playing/now

b. sad/TV program

c. nice/food/New Zealand

d. easy/subject/at school

e. interesting/place/New Zealand

f. dangerous/sport/at school/on television

g. important/person/your country

h. big/lake/New Zealand

i. high/mountain/world

18. Find a partner and tell each other your: age, height, number of brothers and sisters, time you have spent in New Zealand.

Find a new partner and do the same. Then compare the details from each of the students and present a comparison to the class. For example: *A is taller than B, but B has more brothers and sisters. A has been in New Zealand longer than B.*

19. Look at the pairs of photos. Discuss them with a partner using adjectives of comparison. Then write the adjectives in the space.

a. _____

b. _____

English Zone Elementary Student Book

APPLICATION

20. Form groups of three: person A reads about Dunedin; person B reads about Tauranga; person C reads about Palmerston North.

21. In your group of three fill in the chart below.

	size	population	rainfall	max temp.
Dunedin				
Tauranga				
Palmerston North				

Dunedin

Dunedin is situated in Otago in the South Island of New Zealand. It has the largest land area of any New Zealand city (3 350 sq km) and has a population of 120 000. It is a cool city with the average maximum temperature being only 14.75°C and an average rainfall of 660 mm per year.

Tauranga

Tauranga is in the Bay of Plenty region on the east coast of the North Island of New Zealand. It has a small land area of only 12 742 hectares. It has a population of 90 906. It is a warm place to live with an average maximum temperature of 18.3°C, and an average rainfall of 1 200 mm per year.

Palmerston North

Palmerston North is situated on the Manawatu River in the North Island of New Zealand. It has a land area of 32 594 hectares and a population of 73 122. It has a moderate climate. Its average maximum temperature is 16.9°C and an average rainfall of 960 mm per year.

22. Write sentences comparing the three cities. Ensure you relate one city to another and then to both of the other cities. Make sure that you use both superlative and comparative adjectives.

Example: *Tauranga has a larger population than Palmerston North, but Dunedin has the largest population of the three cities.*

Unit 6   Good, Better, Best

23. You have been asked to talk to a group of students from your home country who want to come to study in New Zealand.

They have a choice of the three cities above. Write down what you would tell them about New Zealand as a country and about schools in New Zealand in comparison with schools in your country. Also explain to them what it would be like living in these cities. Use the table, photos and any other information you have about these cities.

Weight and Height comparisons

Name of student	Weight	Height
John	60 kg	160 cm

24. Answer the following questions about your home country.

a. What is its population?
b. What is its average temperature?
c. How big is it in area?
d. What is its average rainfall?

25. Collect bathroom scales and a metre ruler from your teacher. Weigh and measure the height of ten volunteer students in your class and record their weight and height on a table on the board.

a. Who is the tallest person you measured?
b. Who is the shortest?
c. Who is the heaviest person you weighed?
d. Who is the lightest person you weighed?
e. Write some sentences about these ten students. For example: *John is taller than Mary, but Mark is the tallest of the ten students*.

26. Survey the class and ask them the population of their home town. Record these figures in a table and draw a bar graph showing the name and population of each person's home town. Write five sentences comparing the size of the places using both comparison and superlative adjectives.

Home town survey

Student	Home Town	Country	Population

65

REVISION

27. Measure the foot length of every student in the class in centimetres.

Then draw a series of footprints on a sheet of paper from smallest to largest with the names of the student inside the footprints. Write three sentences which sum up the information you have recorded.

_____

_____

_____

28. Write the comparative and superlative forms of the following adjectives.

Adjective	Comparative Adjective	Superlative Adjective
happy	*happier*	*happiest*
famous	*more famous*	*most famous*
a. sad		
b. busy		
c. soft		
d. serious		
e. active		
f. high		
g. easy		
h. pretty		
i. funny		

29. Write out the correct sentence in each pair.

a. Today is more hot than yesterday.
   Today is hotter than yesterday.

b. I'm shorter than my brothers.
   I'm more short than my brothers.

c. I'm the most tall boy in the class.
   I'm the tallest boy in the class.

d. He's the most bad writer in the class.
   He's the worst writer in the class.

e. She's prettier than her friend.
   She's prettyer than her friend.

30. Look at the list of words below and write down what you think they mean without using a dictionary.

Then use your dictionary to check the meaning that you have written. Correct your answer if necessary.

a. rainfall _____

b. climate _____

c. population _____

d. modern _____

e. old-fashioned _____

f. average _____

g. moderate _____

h. pollution _____

i. strict _____

GRAMMAR

Adjectives describe the qualities of people, things and places. **Comparative adjectives** are used when we compare two things. For example: *Peter is taller than Jim*.

Form: *er* is added to one-syllable words, and to two-syllable words ending with 'y'. For example: *Short/shorter, pretty/prettier*.

Longer adjectives become comparatives by adding *more*. For example: *beautiful/more beautiful*.

In a comparison using comparative adjectives, we use *than* before the second part of the comparison. For example: *Kim is shorter than Yuqi*.

Superlative adjectives are used when we compare three or more things. For example: *He is the tallest boy in the class*.

Form: *est* is added to one syllable words and to two syllable words ending with 'y'. For example: *Short/shortest, pretty/prettiest*.

Longer adjectives become superlatives by adding *most*. For example: *beautiful/most beautiful*.

When using superlative adjectives, *in* or *of* are used to show what is being compared. For example: *She is the youngest in the class. Jong is the shortest of the three boys*.

VOCABULARY

expensive / weight / height / average / rainfall / temperature / tall / light / heavy / life / expectancy / population / pollution / cheap / practical / serious / famous / area / climate / modern

TAPESCRIPT

Tapescript 1

Teacher (T) Quiet everyone. We're going to have a geography quiz now. I am sure you will enjoy this. Get out your textbook. The quickest person to answer each question will get the points. Right, are you ready?

What is the population of Australia? John?

John (J) 19 387 000

T Right – one point to you.

Question 2. hat is the population of Thailand? John – again!

J 63 million.

T Excellent. Another point for you, John.

OK, Question 3. What is the population of Indonesia? Adrian?

Adrian (A) 227 million

T Good, a point for you.

Now there are three answers for the next question, and you can win three points.

What are the life expectancies for the three countries we have studied? Keiko?

Keiko (K) Thailand 69 years, Australia 78 years and Indonesia 66 years.

T Well done! Three points for you Keiko. You're now in the lead.

Now, one final question. Let's see if anyone can get ahead of Keiko?

What are the areas of the three countries Australia, Indonesia and Thailand?

Oooh, this is hard.

John, I think you were first.

J Indonesia is 1 million square kilometres, Thailand is 514 000 square kilometres and Australia is 7.7 million square kilometres.

T Close John. Two are right but one's wrong. You only get two points. Can anyone tell me which country was wrong and the correct figure? Keiko.

K Indonesia has 1.9 million square kilometres.

T Well done. That's right. And, that gives you the most points! Keiko is our winner!

OK, the bell is about to go and this is the last class for the day. So, please tidy up the room and put up the chairs before you go. I'll see you all tomorrow.

Unit 7 — The Fashion of Looking Good

Grammar: Present continuous tense: *I'm wearing jeans./Who's wearing jeans?/He's not wearing jeans.* Possessive pronouns: *Her dress/his shoes/their school ball.* Apostrophe to indicate possession: *Bob's dog/Anne's sunglasses.*

Vocabulary: Clothes: *shoes/jacket/skirt/tie.* Fabric: *denim/cotton/silk.* Adjectives to describe people: *blonde/tall/slim/blue eyes.* Fashion: *brocade/model/scruffy.*

STARTER

1. Look at the photos and answer the questions.

a. Describe the clothing worn by the Maori.

_____

b. What nationality are the ladies who are wearing the white aprons?

_____

c. Describel the national dress of your country.

_____

2. Look at the Grammar section and then write sentences which are true for yourself using the present continuous tense.

Example: *I am not wearing school uniform.*

a. I _____ studying.

b. I _____ doing maths.

c. I _____ using a dictionary.

d. It _____ snowing.

e. The teacher _____ talking.

f. My friend _____ watching TV.

g. We _____ going to a party.

Unit 7   The Fashion of Looking Good

3. Write six sentences to describe the woman in her ball gown, saying what she looks like and what she is wearing and holding.

Use the present simple or the present continuous tense in your sentences. For example: *She has blonde hair. She is holding some flowers*.

a. _____
b. _____
c. _____
d. _____
e. _____
f. _____

4. Look at the photograph of each person in the photograph and write down a description of what each person is wearing.

a.
b.
c.
d.

a. _____
b. _____
c. _____
d. _____

5. Look at the picture of the boy, girl and their dog and write an answer to each question using personal pronouns.

Example: Who does the dog belong to? *It's his dog*.

a. Whose is the discman? _____
b. Whose is the bike? _____
c. Whose are the sunglasses? _____
d. Whose is the ball? _____

6. Select someone to collect something from each student in the class and put it on a table at the front of the room.

With the collector at the front of the room, ask and answer questions about the items on the table.

Example: *Is this Xiao Wei's? No it's Mark's. Whose is this pen? It's mine.*

7. Put the correct word from the box into the gaps. There could be more than one correct answer.

my   mine   yours   your   our   ours   her   hers
his   their   theirs   who's   whose

Example: This is *my* new book.

a. Those shoes are _____.
b. _____ pencil case is this?
c. I am going to visit _____ school.
d. Our school is bigger than _____
e. Is this _____ dog?
f. I think this discman is _____.
g. _____ going to the school ball?

8.

a. Choose a partner and sit opposite each other. Write down what your partner is wearing.

b. With a different partner carefully look at what he/she is wearing but write nothing down. Now sit with your back to that person and write down what he/she is wearing and what he/she looks like. No peeking! For example: *She has long blonde hair and blue eyes and she is wearing a blue skirt and a white top.*

69

English Zone Elementary Student Book

LISTENING

9. Look at the photos of the students at the school ball as you listen to Tapescript 1, then answer the questions.

a. What sort of suit is Wang wearing?

_____

b. How many boys in the group photo are wearing bow ties?

_____

c. What did Harris forget to do?

_____

d. Are all the girls wearing ball gowns?

_____

e. What is the name of the student on the far right of the group photo?

_____

f. What is the reason Michael gives for taking photos?

_____

10. Listen to the tape again and look at Tapescript 1. Write down, or underline, the examples of the present continuous tense that you hear. Be careful. Not every word with –ing is an example of the present continuous tense.

11. Listen to Tapescript 2 and say whether the items below are Mariko's or Xu Ran's.

	Mariko	Xu Ran
football		
boots		
violin		
guitar		
art folder		
book (novel)		
movie tickets		

Unit 7   The Fashion of Looking Good

READING

a. b.

12. Match the pictures with the description.

a. Evening wear which is free flowing is appearing in fashions this year. This model is wearing a silk and chiffon, tightly fitting pastel coloured dress which flairs at the bottom to flow with the wind. This is accompanied by a silk scarf of the same material which is used to accentuate the movement as the model walks. Her shoes are metallic silver to match her skirt.

b. Reflecting the Polynesian style Oliver is dressed for summer. Her long flowing dress has a train which she carries. This is contrasted with a halter-neck top made of flowers to represent the lei. Her matching pink flower behind the ear adds a welcoming feature to this outfit.

c. d.

c. The model is wearing black leggings, with a black and white top that is exposing her stomach and a brief black skirt. White casual soft shoes complete the black-white effect.

d. This model is dressing for spring in a thin red evening dress. Her dress contrasts nicely with the black shoes and bag.

13. Write out the examples of the present continuous tense used in the descriptions above.

_____

_____

_____

_____

14. Read the information about Zambesi and answer the questions.

Zambesi

Zambesi was established in 1979. It is owned by Elisabeth and Neville Findlay. It was started by designer Elisabeth Findlay who still directs production of the collections. The label has grown to be an internationally competitive design label. Zambesi has stores in Australia and New Zealand. The New Zealand stores are in Auckland and Wellington.

a. When was Zambesi established?

b. Who owns Zambesi?

c. What do you think Zambesi is?

d. In what two countries can you find Zambesi stores?

e. In what two New Zealand cities are there Zambesi stores?

71

WRITING

15. Look at the photos and write a description of the traditional dresses and say what country they are from.

16. School uniforms are traditional, although not a national dress.

Compare the difference between school uniforms in your country and school uniforms in New Zealand.

17. Write a detailed description of Divad and Paula from NZ Fashion Week, describing their physical features and the clothes that they are wearing.

What is your opinion of what they are wearing? Would you wear these clothes? Visit <www.nzfashionweek.com> to see more NZ fashion.

_____
_____
_____
_____

Divad   Paula

SPEAKING

18. Make a list of fashion trends that are around at the moment.

For example: dreadlocks, blonde hair for Asian teenagers, pierced eyebrows and tongues, spiked hair, gothic clothing, skatey clothing, pointy-toed shoes.

19. Ask everyone in the class what they think of an aspect of current fashion.

For example: hipster jeans, dyed hair colour. Ask each student whether they are already wearing this fashion or whether they would wear it if they had the chance.

20. Record the answers in a table and then rank the fashions from most popular to least popular.

21. In small groups discuss the following: What is a fashion statement? Why do some people choose to make fashion statements?

Comments on current fashion

Fashion statement	Person 1	Person 2	Person 3
pierced eyebrows	I think, terrible!	cool	hurts too much

English Zone Elementary Student Book

APPLICATION

Debbie

John

Abbie

22. Describe what the three children are wearing and what they are going to do while wearing those clothes.

Debbie _____

Abbie _____

John _____

23. Collect an outline of a person from your teacher and draw on the appropriate clothes for either a sporting activity, or a party, or a ball. Write a description of what you have drawn.

24. Conduct a survey amongst students in your school asking whether or not they think school students should wear uniform. Collect a page from your teacher to list your results and write some conclusions.

25. Read through the Grammar section about possessive pronouns, then fill the gaps in the following conversation with possessive pronouns.

Example:

A Do you like *my* new shirt?

B Yes, but *mine* is just as nice for wearing to the movies.

A Bother! I have lost _____ sports socks. My teacher will be upset.

B Would you like to borrow _____. _____ mother won't mind.

A That would be great. I meant to put _____ in _____ bag, but I forgot.

Unit 7   The Fashion of Looking Good

A   What time does _____ team have practice tonight? Is it 5 pm or 7 pm?

B   It must be 5 pm, because James said _____ team has a practice at 7 pm.

A   OK. I'll see you there and I'll give you back _____ socks then.

26. Find a partner and complete the following activities.

a. Decide whether you are going to talk about a school ball, a dress-up party, or a very formal traditional celebration.

b. Describe to your partner exactly what you would wear.

c. Write a description of what your partner has told you.

d. Try to draw the clothing your partner would be wearing.

27. Say what is wrong with the people in the pictures.

a. _____

b. _____

c. _____

d. _____

REVISION

28. Look around you and complete the following sentences using present continuous tense.

a. The students _____ reading books.

b. We _____ watching a video.

c. The teacher _____ sitting down.

d. Students _____ sitting in groups.

e. Some students _____ standing outside.

29. Write a description of your teacher, saying what he/she looks like and what he/she is wearing.

30. Look at the sketch above and answer the following questions.

a. Who does the walking stick belong to?

b. Whose bag is it?

c. What is the child doing?

d. Who does the kite belong to?

e. Whose pet is the puppy?

75

31. Choose the correct word to fill the gaps.

a. That is *their/theirs* teacher.
b. Please give me *my/mine* book.
c. That book is *my/mine*.
d. I am going to *our/ours* place.
e. That puppy is *our/ours*.

32. What are the people in the photo about to do? How do you know?

33. Choose the correct form of the verb in these sentences.

a. I *eat/am eating* breakfast at 7.30am every day.
b. The girl *runs/is running* to catch the bus.
c. The students at our school *wearing/wear* school uniform to school.
d. The dog *has/is having* the ball in its mouth.
e. We *have/are having* meat and potatoes for dinner every night in New Zealand.
f. In my country we *have/are having* rice every day.
g. The students *are studying/study* for exams at the moment.
h. The students *study/are studying* much harder in my country.
i. He *gets/is getting* a ride home today.
j. He *gives/is giving* us a ride home every day.

GRAMMAR

Present continuous tense

The present continuous tense describes something that happens over a limited period of time. It is formed by the present of the verb to be + verb ending –ing.

Example:

I am coming, I'm coming, you/we/they are coming, he/she/it is coming.

Am I coming? Are they/you/we coming? Is he/she/it coming?

I'm not coming. They/we/you aren't coming. He/she/it isn't coming.

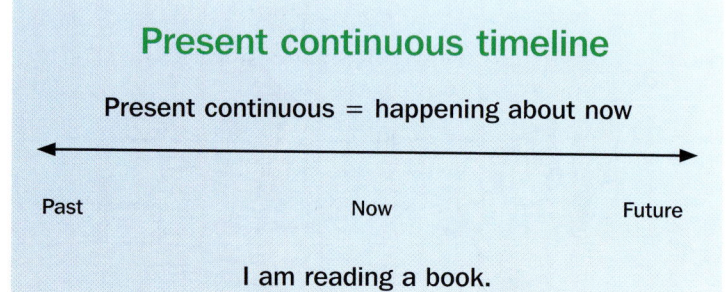

Present continuous timeline

Present continuous = happening about now

Past ←――――――――― Now ―――――――――→ Future

I am reading a book.

Possession

The possessive personal pronoun tells you who something belongs to.

Me becomes *my/mine*. You becomes *your/yours*. He becomes *his*, she becomes *hers*, it becomes *its*, we becomes *our/ours*, they becomes *their/theirs*. Example: *That is their house. This house is theirs.*

When naming the person or thing that owns an object we use *apostrophe + s ('s)*. Example: *the dog's ball/the girl's sunglasses*.

NOTE: It's means it is and NOT belongs to it.

VOCABULARY

ball (school ball) / ball gown / dinner suit / discman / serious / satin / velvet / suede / fashion / brocade / metallic / model / traditional / piercing / scruffy

TAPESCRIPTS

Tapescript 1

Michael Can I see your ball photos? I haven't got mine yet and I'd really like to see what we looked like.

Wang Sure, it was great fun wasn't it? I really enjoyed getting dressed up!

Michael Yes, and the girls looked great! Really old though!

Wang So did we. Older than we look in school uniform anyway. Here you are. I've only got a few with me. The rest are at home.

Michael Look at the one of me with Toni. We look so serious. I love the blue dress she's wearing. I look funny wearing a suit, but not as funny as you do Wang, in your dinner suit and bow tie.

Wang I really like my tie. Doesn't Mai look beautiful wearing that red dress?

Michael She does look good, but it wasn't really a dress. It was a skirt and a red top with a funny thing wrapped around her arms.

Wang That's a shawl I think. It's to keep her a bit warmer. Her top only had straps at the back.

Michael We look good as a group. All the girls look beautiful wearing their ball gowns.

Wang We look pretty good in our suits.

Michael Yes, the boys in dinner suits look the best. Even with the bow ties!

Wang You're right. I wonder why Harris didn't give his partner some flowers. The girls look great with the flowers on their dresses.

Michael It's typical of him, he's always forgetting something!

Wang Anyway, we all had a great time and these photos will help us remember the night!

Michael Well, that's why we take them. I'm off to collect mine. Thanks for showing me yours. See you later!

Wang Bye.

Tapescript 2

Xu Ran What are you doing after school today?

Mariko I am planning to go to soccer practice and then I'm going home to read my book. It's the first real book I've read in English and I'm really enjoying it. What about you?

Xu Ran I have to finish my art assignment and then I am hoping that Jack will give me a guitar lesson.

Mariko Ugh! I forgot. I am playing the violin in tomorrow's concert, so I will do some practice as well.

Xu Ran Well, I guess that means you're too busy to go to a movie with me.

Mariko Yes, sorry. Not tonight. Perhaps we can go next weekend.

Xu Ran That's a thought, but as I've got the tickets I might find someone else to go with.

Mariko Well, I might be able to fit it in. Ring me later. Bye for now.

Xu Ran Bye!

Unit 8 — Working for a Living

Grammar: Revision of present simple and present continuous tenses, questions and negatives: He's a pilot. He flies a plane. Is he flying a plane now? No, he's eating dinner.

Vocabulary: Occupations: pilot/nurse/chef/teacher.

STARTER

a. _____

b. _____

c. _____

d. _____

e. _____

f. _____

g. _____

h. _____

i. _____

j. _____

k. _____

1. Label each photo with the name of the job from the list below.

mechanic   police officer   tow-truck driver   security officer   street sweeper   boat officer

kitchen hand   physical education teacher   builders   sailors   chef

78

Unit 8   Working for a Living

2. What are the people in each photo doing?

a. *He's sweeping the street.*
b. _____
c. _____
d. _____
e. _____
f. _____
g. _____
h. _____
i. _____
j. _____
k. _____

3. Draw a line to match the occupation with the activity.

doctor	cuts hair
dentist	cooks in a restaurant
air steward	treats sick people
builder	serves drinks in a bar
plumber	works on people's teeth
chef	treats sick animals
pilot	builds new buildings
veterinarian	fixes taps, pipes etc.
barman	looks after passengers in a plane
hairdresser	flies a plane

4. Write sentences about James using the information in the profile.

James Brown
Occupation: lawyer
Age: 34 years
Country: New Zealand
City: Rotorua
Marital status: married
Family: wife, one daughter aged two years
Free time: running and going on outings with his family

Example: *He's a lawyer.*
a. He's _____
b. He has _____
c. He lives _____
d. He likes _____
e. He goes _____

5. Read the advertisement for a polytechnic course and answer the questions below.

A Qualification in Fashion

A practical course for people who wish to work in the fashion industry. This course can be done by studying at home whilst working in another job. The world of fashion is growing in New Zealand and is becoming very competitive. If you are dreaming of becoming a fashion designer, this qualification is for you.

a. Who is this course for?
b. Do you have to go to classes to study?
c. What is happening to the world of fashion in New Zealand?
d. Write down the examples of the present continuous tense in this passage.
e. Write down the examples of the present simple tense in this passage.

English Zone Elementary Student Book

6. Write sentences saying what the people in the photos are doing.

a.

b.

c.

d.

e.

a. _____
b. _____
c. _____
d. _____
e. _____

LISTENING

7. Listen to the three people on the tape talking about their jobs and write down what they do, what they like about their job, what they dislike and what they do in their spare time.

	The job	Likes about the jo
Pip		
Gareth		
Deborah		

8. Listen to the tape a second time and answer the following questions

a. What does Pip like doing in her spare time?
b. Why is she such a busy person?
c. Why does she feel that she is lucky?
d. What do you think a second chef is?
e. Why doesn't he have much social life?
f. What is his dream?
g. Why did Deborah take a break from university?
h. What is telemarketing?
i. What is commission?
j. Does she like telemarketing? How do you know?

Unit 8 Working for a Living

READING

Prereading

Success varies depending on the field of study or work. Being successful in business may be measured in profits or how big the business grows. In charity work, success may be seen as the number of people you help. In art, it may be a painting or a song that people like. When people are very successful and gain a lot of publicity they are often referred to as 'tall poppies'. They are taller than the other successful people, they are more noticed by the public. Often these tall people received negative reactions from some people in society and the press, thus the saying, 'Cutting the tall poppy down to size'. In other words not letting the very successful people get too much above the other poppies in the field.

Discuss tall poppies and what happens to tall poppies in New Zealand. How are high achievers treated in your country?

Growing tall poppies is the way to nurture our economy

… Jenene is a 24 year-old businesswoman who set up the hugely successful nzgirl.co.nz website, an online magazine dedicated to 15–29 year-olds. The site records up to 3300 users a day. Leaving school at 16, Jenene entered the workforce armed with the motivation to succeed and a gut feeling that her product was the way to do it. Jenene now offers her services as a marketer, specialising in the teen market.

their jobs	
Dislikes about the job	Spare time activities

9. Listen to the tape again and write down the following:

a. Examples of the present continuous tense that you hear.

b. Examples of the present simple tense you hear.

<www.nzgirl.co.nz>

10. Read *Growing tall poppies is the way to nurture our economy* and answer the following questions.

a. What business did Jenene set up?
b. Did Jenene go to university before she started her business?
c. How do we know that the website is successful?
d. What do you think this website is about?

Prereading

With your teacher discuss the meaning of entrepreneur? Do you know any stories of successful entrepreneurs?

11. Read this extract and answer the following questions.

Wattie's Tomato Sauce

… James Wattie liked tomato sauce. He started making it in his Hastings home. He soon discovered that the rest of New Zealand liked tomato sauce too. Sir James Wattie took what he had, and turned it into what we needed.

Entrepreneurship is about getting down to hard work. It's not about a lucky break. James Wattie grew tomatoes, picked tomatoes, processed tomatoes, packaged tomatoes, sold tomatoes …

So what makes an entrepreneur? What turns a crazy idea into a successful business? It's about taking what we have, and turning it into what we need. It's about passion. It's about determination. It's about risk. It's about tomatoes and baskets and boats. It's about New Zealanders. It's about tomorrow.

a. What product did Sir James Wattie produce?
b. Did Sir James have a lot of help when he first started making tomato sauce?
c. What do entrepreneurs have to do?
d. What is passion?
e. Did Sir James have to spend a lot of money to start his business?

WRITING

12. Complete the sentences and answer the questions.

Example: Tomiko is a *doctor*. Is she operating now? *No, she's eating lunch*.

a. Mark is a _____ . Is he working in the bar now?
_____

b. Jason is a _____ . Is he working as a lawyer now?
_____

c. Yoshi is a _____ . Is he teaching now?
_____

d. Seona is a _____ . Is she looking after sick people now?
_____

e. Mae is a _____ . Is she studying now?
_____

SPEAKING

13. Read Jason's letter and then write a letter of application for yourself for a job at a shop or business where you would like to be employed. Use the telephone book or a business directory to find the address to write to.

---

12 Smith St
Rotorua
New Zealand

6th February 2003

The Manager
Chicken Heaven
Amohau Street
Rotorua

Dear Sir/Madam,

I would like to apply for a job in your restaurant. I am 17 years old and will be leaving school in two weeks time.

I have been in New Zealand for three years and can speak English well. I have studied cooking at school and know the rules regarding working with food.

I can come for an interview any time.

Please contact me on my cell phone: 021 408296.

Yours faithfully,
Jason Wang
Jason Wang

---

14. What job do the following people do?

a. I wear a white uniform.
   I work with people.
   The people are often quite unwell.
   I often work in a hospital.
   What am I? _____

b. I don't wear a uniform.
   I work longer hours than most people know about.
   I do a lot of reading and writing.
   I work with children.
   What am I? _____

15. Write three to four 'What am I?' clues and ask two other people in the room to guess what job you are describing.

16. Talk to the other students about their parents' jobs.

a. Find a partner you don't know very well and ask him/her about his/her parents' jobs. Ask what their occupation is, what work they have to do, and what they wear while they are at work. Write the answers in a table.

b. Join up with another pair of students and tell them about the information you have gained from your partner.

Example: *A's father is a bank clerk. He works with people and money all day and he wears a suit to work.*

17. Survey all the students in your class and write down what job they would like to do when they leave school.

Job survey

Name	Sex	Nationality	Preferred job	Why this career
Mae	F	Chinese	chef	likes cooking

English Zone Elementary Student Book

APPLICATION

Job Description

Teaching Position: English Teacher

Time: Full-time

Location: Rotorua Boys High School, Rotorua

General statement of duties:

To teach English skills and literature to a range of students from Year 9 to 12. Some teaching of English to Asian students with few English skills may be required but will be limited to 10% of the teaching load. Other duties include sport and helping with monitoring a small group of 20 students and their pastoral care.

Specific duties include:

i. Teaching 6 classes of English of 40 minutes each for 5 lessons each week.

ii. Teaching 1 ESOL class of 6 students 4 times a week for 30 minutes.

iii. Pastoral care of a form group of 20 students.

iv. Undertaking adequate teaching preparation to ensure that 80% of students at all levels pass English; in particular the Year 12 pass rate is 80% or better. This does not include the ESOL students.

v. Coaching sport on a Saturday morning from between 8–10am and finishing between 12–3pm.

vi. Keeping careful records of student performance is mandatory and being able to account this to school administration and parents is essential.

vii. Attending weekly staff meetings after school hours and a weekly department meeting at a lunch-time.

Discuss job descriptions with your teacher.

18. Imagine that your school wants to employ a new ESOL teacher. Brainstorm and record on the board all the things that you think that teacher must be prepared to do.

For example: *They must teach ESOL classes. They should help ESOL students with their other subjects.*

19. Write down and discuss job descriptions.

a. In pairs, select two or three different jobs and write job descriptions for the job.

b. Join up with another pair and read out your job descriptions. Can they guess what job your description is for?

c. Tell each other if anything has been missed out of the job descriptions.

20. Read the profiles of the people below and match them with a job which would suit them best.

John

A 17 year-old boy who likes working outside. He has left school before completing Year 12, but wants to learn about looking after animals, and perhaps shearing sheep and milking cows. He is working for friends of his parents but wants to move further away from home.

Li Mei

A 23 year-old design student who wants to work in the area of art and design. She particularly enjoys designing clothes and seeing them worn by models at fashion shows.

Jong

A 22 year-old new graduate who has just finished a business degree. He has lived in New Zealand for six years and wants to gain some business experience here before returning to China, where he comes from. He is working as a barman at present, but is keen to get what he calls 'a proper job'.

Sandra

A 25 year-old graduate who wants to travel and enjoys working with people. She has a nursing degree but does not want to work with sick people in a hospital. At the moment she is nursing in private homes, but she thinks this is very boring.

Assistant manager wanted

Manager of a small company requires a young manager to assist in the marketing department and representing the company at business shows.

a.

Airline attendant needed

Airline attendant needed by airline trying to open new Pacific routes.

b.

Farm assistant needed

Farm assistant needed for modern dairy farm midway between Auckland and Rotorua.

c.

Trainee fashion designer

Fashion house needs young trainee designer to assist in building new range of young people's clothes.

d.

REVISION

21. Underline or write out all the examples of the present continuous tense that were used in the descriptions of people in the Application section.

22. For each of the photographs, say what the person's job is and what they are doing now.

Example: *He is a courier. He is unloading a parcel.*

a. _____

b. _____

c. _____

d. _____

e. _____

f. _____

g. _____

23. Correct these sentences.

Example: A doctor looks after people who have sore teeth.
No, he/she doesn't, he/she looks after people who are sick.

a. An airline steward looks after children who are sick.
_____

b. A nurse works on an aeroplane.
_____

c. A gardener helps you keep your house clean.
_____

d. A business manager packs boxes in the warehouse.
_____

e. A 'tall poppy' is someone who doesn't achieve anything.
_____

f. A chef serves people in a restaurant.
_____

g. A waiter cooks the meals in a restaurant.
_____

h. A librarian works in a shop.
_____

i. A shop assistant works in a factory.
_____

24. Make a list of three things that each of the following people have to do in their jobs.

a. plumber	
b. librarian	
c. taxi driver	
d. gardener	
e. business person	

GRAMMAR

Present simple tense

The present simple tense is most commonly used for a present state, for example: *I am a New Zealander,* or a present habit, for example: *I do ballet on Saturday.*

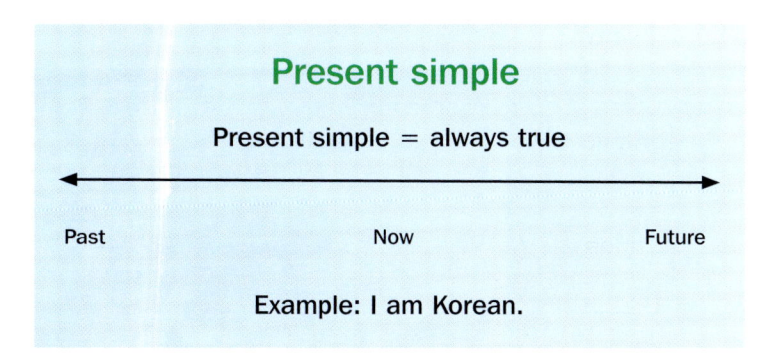

Present simple

Present simple = always true

Past — Now — Future

Example: I am Korean.

Present continuous tense

The present continuous tense is used to describe a temporary event that is happening about now. It is formed by using the verb *to be* and the verb + *ing*.

Details of these forms have been discussed in earlier units of the Student Book and can be referred back to if necessary.

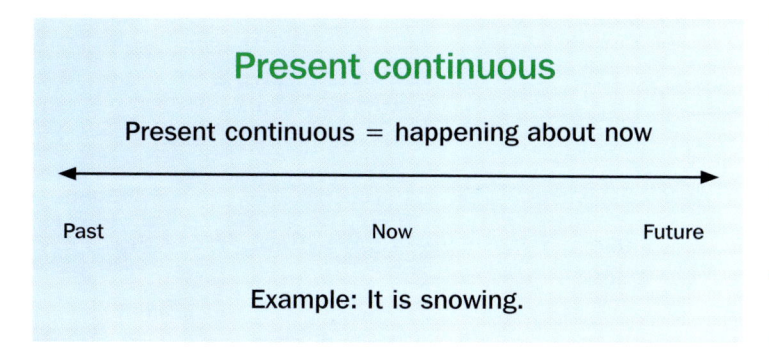

Present continuous

Present continuous = happening about now

Past — Now — Future

Example: It is snowing.

VOCABULARY

nurse / doctor / air / steward / business / person / gardener / taxi driver / chef / tall poppy / entrepreneur / passion / plumber / telemarketing / farm assistant / barman / waiter / factory

TAPESCRIPTS

Tapescript 1: Pip

I'm a 26 year-old English teacher who teaches English at a boys' school in a New Zealand city. The best part of my job is teaching students in the classroom, and the worst parts are the meetings and all the paperwork I have to do. I also have to help with sport or cultural activities outside normal school hours, and this can take a lot of time.

I am a very busy person as I have a small son to look after in between marking and lesson preparation.

In my spare time I like reading and walking and playing netball, but at the moment I don't have a lot of spare time.

However, I am really lucky as, unlike many people, I do enjoy my job!

Tapescript 2: Gareth

I am a 20 year-old chef and I am now working in my first full-time job in a small restaurant in Rotorua. I am second chef, so I spend a lot of time preparing salads and vegetables and I don't get many chances to do the interesting things. I start work at 3pm and finish at about 11pm, so I don't have much social life. I am really missing seeing my friends, but it is good to have an income. On my days off I catch up with my friends, cruise around in my car and watch videos.

I guess the job will get better as I gain more experience. One day I might own my own restaurant and then I will choose what cooking I want to do, and what hours I want to work!

Tapescript 3: Deborah

I am a student with a Bachelor's degree and I am having a break before starting an Honours course. As I am 23 years-old, I am sick of being a student with no money, so I decided I needed a break. To earn some money I am doing a telemarketing job every evening. I am selling medical insurance. I have to sell six packages a night to earn my basic wage and then I get commission for anything extra I sell. It can be very boring, but I am earning quite a lot of money so I will keep doing it until I go back to uni.

At least I now have some spare time to do some leisuretime reading and go out with my friends. I have also started going to the gym regularly and going for long walks on the beach on warm summer evenings.

Unit 9 — Please, Can I Drive the Car?

Grammar: Degrees of obligation: *should, must, have to*. Infinitive of Purpose: *to get/to eat*.
Vocabulary: Vehicles: *cars/buses/trucks*. Rules: *licence/learner/restricted/full*.
Driving procedures and regulations: *give way/turning right*.

STARTER

1. Complete the sentences with *have to*, *must*, *must not*, *should*, *shouldn't* (*must* and *have to* are interchangeable).

Example: You *have to/must* wait until you are 16 years old to get a Learner's Licence.

a. You _____ wear a seat belt when the car is moving.

b. When you buy a car, you _____ have it checked by a mechanic.

c. You _____ pass your driving test before you buy a car.

d. You _____ read the Road Code before sitting your Restricted Licence.

e. You _____ drive in New Zealand until you know the road rules.

f. You _____ have a New Zealand Licence after you have been in the country for one year.

2. Discuss the difference between *should* and *must/have to*. Which of the following things *should* you do, and which things do you *must/have to* do?

Example: You must/have to attend school New Zealand until you are 16 years old.

a. You _____ do all your homework.

b. You _____ contact your friends and parents regularly.

c. You _____ wear a seatbelt in a moving car.

d. You _____ get a licence before you can legally drive a car.

e. You _____ drive at 50 km in built up areas.

f. You _____ keep your room clean and tidy.

3. Answer the following questions, using the infinitive of purpose, so they are true for you.

Refer to the Grammar section to find out more about the infinitive of purpose.

Example: Why did you come to New Zealand? I came to New Zealand to learn English.

a. Why did you choose this school?

b. Why do people learn the Road Code?

c. Why should you wear a seat belt?

d. Why do you drive at 50 km in built-up areas?

e. Why do you need a driver's licence?

f. Why might you go home for a holiday?

g. Why do you go to the supermarket?

h. Why do you go to the Post Office?

4. Write two reasons why you think New Zealand now uses photo driver's licences rather than licences without photos?

5. Write the meaning of each sign in the space underneath it.

a. _____

b. _____

c. _____

d. _____

e. _____

f. _____

g. _____

h. _____

English Zone Elementary Student Book

LISTENING

Prelistening task

The tape includes a talk from a traffic officer about driving a car in New Zealand. He talks about what you have to do before you drive a car in New Zealand, as well as car and driving safety. Have you driven a car in your home country? Have you driven a car in New Zealand? Would you like to be able to drive?

Discuss these questions with other students before listening to the tape.

6. Listen to Tapescript 1 and answer the questions. You may need to play the tape a few times to get all the answers to the questions.

a. Who does the traffic officer say are most likely to have traffic accidents?

b. In what situation should you never drive?

c. Who should check your car?

d. What certificate does your car get after it has been inspected by a mechanic?

e. Can you drive in New Zealand with a driver's licence from your home country?

f. What should you know before you drive a car in New Zealand?

g. What should you do before buying a car from a friend?

h. List four things the traffic officer said drivers should do.

i. List two things the traffic officer said drivers have to do.

7. Listen to Tapescript 2 and answer the questions.

a. Who should the student check with before buying a car?

b. Why will they have to walk to and from the car yards?

c. Why do you think S2 is being so bossy?

d. Why do you think S2 wanted to do things properly?

e. List five things you should do before buying a car. (Use information from both tapescripts.)

READING

8. Carefully read the following traffic situations. Draw an intersection and mark on it two cars and identify who gives way to who for each of the points below.

a. If you are at an intersection where two roads cross, and you want to turn left, give way to all vehicles coming towards you and those turning right.

b. If you are at an intersection where two roads cross and you are turning right, give way to all right-turning vehicles coming from your right.

c. If you are at an intersection where two roads cross, with no give way or stop signs, and you are going straight through, you must give way to all vehicles coming straight through from your right.

d. If you are at an intersection where two roads cross wanting to turn right, and another vehicle approaches you on the same road wanting to turn right, no one has to give way because they will not cross each other's path. It is safe to turn.

9. Identify which car gives way in each picture.

a. _____
b. _____
c. _____
d. _____
e. _____

a.
b.
c. 
d. 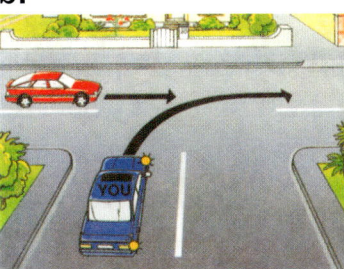
e. 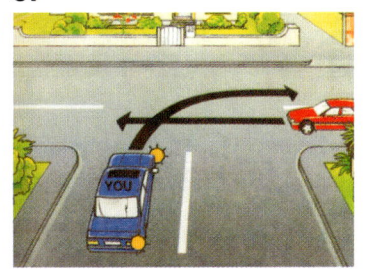

10. Read the following information about the Graduated Driver Licensing System and answer the following questions.

The Graduated Driver Licensing System is designed to build your driving and road safety skills as you progress through the system. You must be 15 years old before you can apply for a licence.

There are three stages of the licence:

1. Learner licence.

You must not drive on your own when you have a learner licence – the person with you must have had a full licence for two years and be at least 20 years old or older. You must not any drink alcohol and drive.

2. Restricted licence

You must not drink any alcohol before driving. You must not drive between 10 pm and 5 am without a supervisor, as for the learner licence. You can only take your parents, spouse, children or a supervisor as passengers.

3. Full licence

You must obey all the laws pertaining to driving, but there are no additional restrictions on your driving.

As you pass each stage you are given a new licence which you must carry with you whenever you are driving a car.

a. How many stages are there in the licensing system?

b. Why is there a graduated system?

c. How old must you be to apply for a licence?

d. What must you do whenever you are driving a car?

e. Can you drive by yourself when you have a learner licence?

f. During what times do you need a supervisor if you have a restricted licence?

English Zone Elementary Student Book

WRITING

11. Use the internet, copies of the NZ Road Code, and driver education material from your teacher to gain information of the legal requirements for obtaining a licence and driving safely in New Zealand. The Land Transport Safety Authority website is <www.ltsa.gov.nz>.

a. Write a list of things that you must do before obtaining a full licence in New Zealand.

b. Write out six road rules that apply to driving cars in New Zealand.

c. Write out three things that are advisable, but not compulsory, when you think about learning to drive. For example: You should do a defensive driver course.

d. Write down five safety features that must be present on your car.

12. Label the following safety features on the car photos and draw a line from the small photo to the correct place you would find this feature on a car.

Safety features your car must have

headlights   windscreen wipers   safe tyres
mirrors   back light
rear lights indicators   seat belts

a. _____

b. _____

c. _____

d. _____

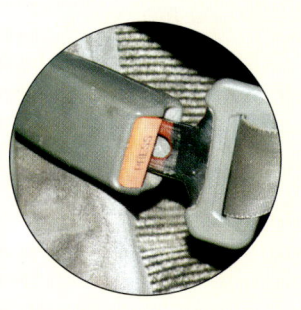

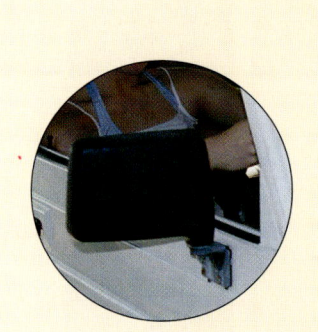

e. _____

f. _____

g. _____

h. _____

92

SPEAKING

> You can drive my car anytime you like as long as you are careful, have a licence, complete a defensive driver course, only drive in daylight, don't drive in the wet or heavy traffic, keep under 50 kph, don't have other kids in the car, don't drink and drive, and keep out of the city centre. Other than that, any time you like!

13. Divide into pairs and collect role-play cards from your teacher. Practise your role-plays together and then come back and present them in front of the whole class.

Remember to use words such as *must* and *have to* if you are playing the parent in the role-play.

Role-play 1

Person A

You are the parent.

Your child has a restricted licence (cannot take friends as passengers or drive after 10 pm).

The car is the family car.

You will not allow your child to break the law.

Person B

You are 16 years old.

You've had a restricted licence for 2 months.

You want to borrow the car to take your friends to a party that finishes at midnight.

You really want to do this, and don't think it is fair that your parents have said no!

Role-play 2

Person A

You are 16 years old and want to buy a car that a boy at school is selling.

It is cheap, but doesn't have a Warrant of Fitness. It needs some work to be really safe on the road.

You have saved up most of the money, but are asking your parents to lend you $200.00.

Person B

You are the parent.

You accept that your child needs a car because you live a long way from school.

You want him/her to buy a roadworthy car that is registered and warranted.

You want him/her to save up and buy it for themselves.

You want your child to look at a number of cars and choose carefully.

English Zone Elementary Student Book

APPLICATION

14. Use the information in the Reading section to say whether the blue car has to give way to the red car in each picture.

a. _____

b. _____

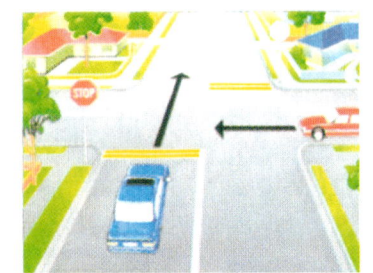

c. _____

d. _____

e. _____

f. _____

g. _____

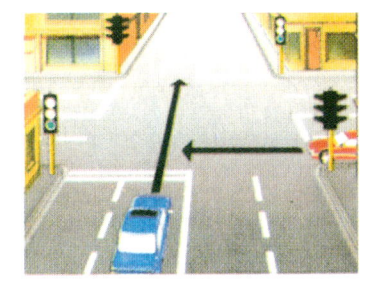

h. _____

15. Read the following information and then write down five things you *must do* and three things it *would be a good idea to do* if you are going to drive in New Zealand.

In New Zealand the open road speed is 100 km/hr and in cities it is normally 50 km/hr. It has been suggested that international students should take one or two years to become familiar with the road rules and road conditions in New Zealand before deciding to get a licence and drive a car. It is also wise to make sure that the people whose cars you are a passenger in, are careful and experienced drivers.

The law states that all drivers and passengers must wear seatbelts whenever the car is moving. It is also compulsory for all cars to be registered and to have a Warrant of Fitness.

When you do buy a car, it is very wise to have it insured.

All drivers must have their licences with them at all times, and you must not drink alcohol when you are about to drive, or while you are driving.

Things you must do

a. _____

b. _____

c. _____

d. _____

e. _____

Things it would be a good idea to do

f. _____

g. _____

h. _____

Unit 9   Please, Can I Drive the Car?

REVISION

16. Write down three stages of the Graduated Driver's Licence System.

a. _____
b. _____
c. _____

17. What are the requirements of the first two stages of a driver's licence?

a. _____
_____

b. _____
_____

18. How fast are you allowed to drive on roads where these signs are displayed?

a. _____   b. _____

c. _____   d. _____

e. _____   f. _____

g. _____   h. _____

19. Fill the gaps with an infinitive of purpose.

Example: *I am going to the shop to buy a copy of the Road Code.*

a. He plans to go into the police station _____ an appointment to sit his licence next week.

b. He's taking the car to the garage _____ a new Warrant of Fitness.

c. He is planning to go to the car yard _____ a new car next week.

d. The Traffic Department is stopping a lot of drivers _____ their licences.

GRAMMAR

Obligation

To express something that you are obliged to do (by law or by rules of an institution) we use *must*, or *have to*, or *have got to*. To express things that are advisable to do we use *should*.

Infinitive of purpose

We use expressions of purpose to explain why? or what for? The infinitive of purpose tells us why something happens. For example: Why did he go to the post office? *To register* his car. I have come to this school *to learn* English. He opened the window *to get* some fresh air.

VOCABULARY

licence / warrant of fitness / learner / restricted / insurance / graduated / government / registration / compulsory / requirement / situation / roadworthy / intersection / vehicle / seatbelt

TAPESCRIPTS

Tapescript 1

Traffic Officer (TO) Thank you for inviting me to talk about driving and the New Zealand laws in regard to driving.

Firstly, I must point out to you that young people in cars are more at risk of having accidents than any other age group. That is why we are very strict about how you obtain a licence and how you drive once you have passed your test.

I will leave you written information about the Graduated Driver Licensing System and how to obtain your licence. I will spend my time talking to you about safety once you are on the road.

Before driving a car in New Zealand, you should read the Road Code and learn the road rules which apply in this country.

Once you have your licence, you should:

* Practise driving with a responsible adult until you both feel that you have good driving skills.
* Only drive at night when it is necessary to do so. Most accidents occur between 9pm and midnight, so try to keep off the roads late at night.
* Avoid taking other young people in the car with you. They can distract you and encourage you to take unnecessary risks.
* Always wear a seatbelt. Insist that your passengers do as well.
* Never drive after drinking alcohol.
* Make sure that your vehicle is completely safe and has been checked by a professional mechanic.

Now, does anyone have any questions?

Student 1 (S1) I have a Chinese drivers licence, do I still need a NZ one?

TO Yes you do. A visitor may use their own licence for up to one year. But, if you are living here, you need to get yourself a NZ licence in that first year. It is very important that you understand the NZ Road Rules. You should study for your restricted licence before you drive a car in New Zealand.

Student 2 (S2) Is it alright to buy a car from a friend or do you have to buy one from a car dealer?

TO You are probably safer to buy a car from a licensed dealer. If you do buy a car from a friend, you should have it checked by a mechanic first to make sure it has a current Warrant of Fitness and Registration.

S2 What's a Warrant of Fitness?

TO It's a certificate that states that your car is safe to drive. No car is allowed to be driven legally on New Zealand roads without a Warrant of Fitness.

I'm sorry, but I've run out of time. I'll leave you to study the Road Code and to read about the Graduated Licensing System. I will be back in a fortnight to test those of you who are ready to sit the Learner Licence Test.

Tapescript 2

Student 1 (S1) My parents have sent me $15 000 and said I can buy a car. Will you come and help me choose one?

Student 2 (S2) Does your school allow you to buy a car? Have you checked with your homestay parents?

S1 Yes, the school says it's OK if my parents and I sign a contract. My homestay parents say it's OK if I go for my New Zealand licence and don't do anything the law says I can't do.

S2 Well, that means we'll have to walk to the car yards and you won't be able to drive until you have your restricted licence. I don't have any sort of licence. You only have a learners now, don't you?

S1 Yes, but I can sit my restricted next week and I'd like to have my own car by then.

S2 OK. I'll come and look with you, but you won't be able to buy one and drive it home as you will need an adult with you in order to drive.

S1 I know that. I just want to look now and bring my homestay father back with me when I have found the car I like.

S2 I'm sorry. I just want to make sure we do things properly. Let's go!

Unit 10 — Yesterday and Today

Grammar: Past simple tense: Regular and irregular verbs, positive sentences, questions and negatives: *I carry/I carried. I was/Were you?/I wasn't. He ran/Did he run?/He didn't run.*

Vocabulary: Stages of life: *born/educated/married/grew up/died.* Daily activities: *worked/bathed/washed/cooked.*

STARTER

Yoshi is a 21 year-old Japanese man who lives in New Zealand. When he was younger, he lived in Japan with his parents and sister and attended school in Tokyo. He arrived in New Zealand when he was 16 years old, attended school there for three years and lived with a homestay family. He then studied at the local polytechnic for two years.

Now he is at university and he is training to be a teacher. He lives in a university hostel and plays rugby and volleyball.

1. Read the information about Yoshi and answer the questions.

a. Fill in the blanks in the following sentence.

When he _____ young he _____ with his parents and sister. Now he _____ in a university hostel.

b. Write down the past tense form of the following verbs in the text:

Present	Past
attend	_____
arrive	_____
study	_____
live	_____

2. When did Yoshi:

a. come to New Zealand? _____
b. live with his parents? _____

3. Where did Yoshi:

a. study in Japan? _____
b. live when he was at school in New Zealand? _____
c. study when he finished school? _____

4. Read the Grammar section on regular past tense verbs, and then write the past tense form of the following verbs. Listen to Tapescript 1 and practise saying the words.

Example: look   *looked*

a. work   _____
b. carry   _____
c. talk   _____
d. start   _____
e. finish   _____
f. travel   _____

g.   ask   _____
h.   help   _____
i.   copy   _____

5. Complete the sentences with *did*, *was*, or *were*.

Example: Where *were* you born?

a. Where _____ you go to school when you were 6 years old?

b. When _____ you come to New Zealand?

c. When _____ you learn to ride a bike?

d. What _____ your favourite leisure activity in your home country?

6. Rewrite these sentences as negatives.

Example: He was late for school this morning.

He *was not* late for school this morning.

a. She came to school by car.

_____

b. He played rugby every Saturday.

_____

c. She went to ballet lessons every Friday.

_____

d. They sat the exam last week.

_____

7. Answer the questions in activity 5 using past tense verbs.

Example: Where were you born? *I was born in Rotorua.*

a. _____

b. _____

c. _____

d. _____

8. Read the passage below and find the past tense form of the following irregular verbs: come, go, find, say, ride. (Check the irregular verb list at the end of this unit if you are not sure.)

Joanna is a secondary school student in New Zealand. She came here two years ago from China and is now attending a girls' school in Rotorua. In China she went to a co-educational school, and when she first arrived she found it quite strange with only girls in her classes. However, when she was asked about it, she said that it was easier to study without boys in her class. In China, she rode a bike to school. But in New Zealand, she walks.

The best book I ever read

The best party I ever went to.

The best meal I ever cooked

The best class I have

The worst thing I've ever done for fun

9. Work in pairs and ask and answer questions about:

a. The best book you have read or video you have seen.
b. The best class you have ever been in.
c. The best party you have ever been to.
d. The worst meal you have ever cooked.
e. The worst fun activity you have ever done.

10. Choose one of the subjects in activity 9 and tell the class about what your partner has told you.

LISTENING

11. Listen to the poem by Ken Nesbitt on Tapescript 2. It is a poem about Martians, living creatures that come from the planet Mars. It is fictional and written to be humorous. Fill in the missing words.

I've recently _____ from Mars
I _____ for several years.
I _____ in Martian motorcars,
_____ Martian souvenirs.

I _____ to Martian movies
and _____ Martian movie stars,
_____ Martian concerts
and _____ Martians play guitars.

I _____ in Martian restaurants
and _____ to Martian schools.
I _____ on Martian tennis courts
and _____ in Martian pools.

I _____ around with Martian girls
and _____ to Martian boys.
I _____ to Martian shopping malls
and _____ with Martian toys.

At last I'm back on planet Earth
from out among the stars.
So why does everyone I see here
act like they're from Mars?

by Ken Nesbitt from 'The Aliens Have Landed'

12. Write down the present tense form of the verbs you have written in the gaps in activity 11.

a. _____   i. _____
b. _____   j. _____
c. _____   k. _____
d. _____   l. _____
e. _____   m. _____
f. _____   n. _____
g. _____   o. _____
h. _____   p. _____

READING

Prereading

Discuss how life has changed in the last seventy years. Brainstorm for a list of things we have now that we didn't have seventy years ago.

13. Read Eileen's account of her childhood, growing up in Christchurch in the 1930s. How many things does she mention that you had thought of? Use the process of skimming, identifying unknown words, checking meaning, rereading.

When I was a child, families spent a lot of time together and they were more important than our friends. We had smaller houses, but big gardens where we played during the day. There was no television, tape decks, CD players, telephones or computers. In the evenings we read books, played games or cards, and listened to the radio. Mothers didn't go out to work as they were busy in the house, and they were always there when we got home from school. We walked to school with our brothers, sisters and friends. It was very safe then, and our parents didn't worry about us. Very few families owned cars, so we travelled by tram or bus, or we walked or rode bikes.

School was very different from today. Our teachers were very strict and strapped us for almost anything. We were very scared of them, and certainly we didn't dare to talk in class. We had 45 to 50 students in each class, and we were all very polite and did exactly as we were told.

There were no supermarkets and each suburb had its

own butchery, bakery, grocery, drapery and dairy, where the owner of the shop was the person who served us. Food did not come in packets, and flour, sugar, etc. were weighed on scales and put into a paper bag. Our milk was delivered by a 'milky' who travelled by horse and cart. He had large cans of milk on the cart and ladled our milk into 'billies' we left on the doorstep or at the gate. We did not have a fridge, so we kept our milk and meat in a cool cupboard called a 'safe'.

Our mothers worked very hard in the house. There were no washing machines or vacuum cleaners. Washing the clothes took a whole day as everything was washed by hand, scrubbed on a scrubbing board and sometimes boiled in a copper. When it was clean, it was put through a mangle to get rid of the water, and then everything was hung outside on the line. A wet washing day was a disaster, and we had wet washing hanging around the house for several days.

Although this sounds like a hard life, we were all very happy and our childhoods seemed to last for a lot longer than they do for children today.

14. Use the following headings and write down the differences between life in the 1930s and life today. Use full sentences and past tense verbs.

a. Housework
b. Transport
c. School
d. Shopping
e. Entertainment

15. Find the past tense form of the following verbs in the passage.

Example: spend   *spent*

a. read   _____
b. listen   _____
c. play   _____
d. strap   _____
e. keep   _____
f. wash   _____
g. scrub   _____
h. travel   _____
i. have   _____

WRITING

16. Write a sentence using the past tense saying what the boy in 'Back from Mars' was doing in each picture.

Example:

a.

b.

c.

d.

Example: *He rode Martian motor cars.*

a. _____
b. _____
c. _____
d. _____

17. Write about one of your parents or grandparents describing their life as a child and their life now.

18. Put the past tense form of the verb in brackets into the gaps.

Last New Year I (stay) _____ in New Zealand instead of going home. I (want) _____ to see how the New Year is celebrated in New Zealand. On New Year's Eve we (do) _____ nothing special, except some of the young people (have) _____ some drinks and (wait) _____ for midnight before they (go) _____ to bed. New Year's Day (is) _____ really boring. The family (go) _____ to the beach for a barbeque.

This (is) _____ very different from New Year in Japan. I (go) _____ home this year and as usual we (spend) _____ New Year's Eve cleaning and decorating the house. My whole family (go) _____ to the temple at midnight and (listen) _____ to all the bells ringing. On New Year's Day all my cousins, uncles and aunts, and grandparents (come) _____ to my house. We (give) _____ each other presents and (have) _____ a big traditional meal together.

I think New Year in Japan is much more exciting than New Year in New Zealand.

SPEAKING

19. Collect a chart from your teacher and write down what other students in the class tell you about what they did:

a. yesterday morning

b. last weekend

c. last month

d. on their last holiday

e. last time they were at home

20. Find a partner and tell them about:

a. when you first met your best friend

b. when you first met your homestay mother, hostel master/matron

c. your first day at school in New Zealand

d. your first day at school in your home country

21. Prepare a two-minute speech on one of the following topics. You may find photographs or old documents to show during your speech.

* signing of the Treaty of Waitangi
* history of rugby in New Zealand
* Lady Diana Spencer
* development of telecommunications from 1900–2003

Follow these steps to prepare your speech.

a. Go to the library or use the Internet to gather some information on the topic you choose.

b. Organise your information so your speech has an introduction, a middle part to develop your ideas, and a conclusion which summarises your points.

c. Remember that you are speaking about events in the past, so you must use the past tense. Once you have written your speech, practise reading it aloud. When you feel you can deliver your speech without reading from your notes, present it to your class. Remember that to make your speech interesting you must look at your audience and vary your voice.

d. You may use pictures, PowerPoint or motion pictures to make your speech more interesting.

APPLICATION

22. Write a 100–150 word account of your own childhood. Follow these steps to write up your account.

a. List the places you liked to go to, things you did, important people in your past.

b. Group sections of your life into two or three groups for paragraphs. This may be chronologically, but it could be based on the important things in your life.

c. Write up your account.

d. Use a dictionary to check your spelling.

e. Ask your teacher to check your work.

f. Write a good copy (with a photo if you have one) to be displayed on the wall.

23. Interview a parent helper at your school.

a. Choose an adult who has been working in New Zealand for more than ten years and ask how things have changed in her/his work in the last 10–20 years.

b. Ask about the type of work done, the pay, the hours of work.

c. Write a paragraph about what you have been told.

24. Draw a timeline for your life. Divide it into the following sections:

0-2 years

2-5 years

5-10 years

10-15 years

15-18+ years.

In each section write at least two important things that happened to you.

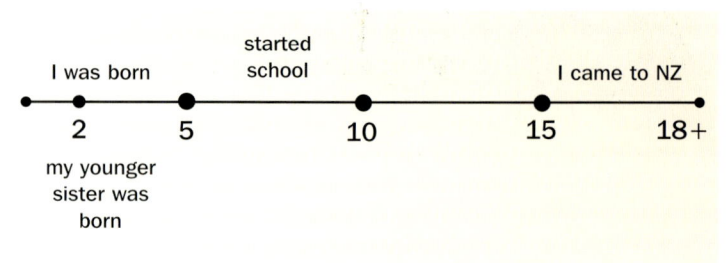

25. Label each of these objects.

a.  _____   b. _____

c.  _____   d. _____

e.  _____   f. _____

REVISION

26. Listen to Tapescript 3 about fireworks and answer the questions.

a. Why was December 31st 1999 an important day?
b. Did the speaker let off any fireworks?
c. How did she know what other countries did?
d. What happened in Gisborne?
e. Why was Gisborne chosen for the official traditional celebration?

27. Write down what you remember about the following:

a. What you did on December 31st 1999.
b. Four things you did in 1999.

28. Tick the correct sentence from each pair.

a. Did you see Keiko last week?
   Did you saw Keiko last week?
b. Where you go to school in China?
   Where did you go to school in China?
c. Did she get a new bike?
   Did she got a new bike?
d. She carried the little boy in her arms.
   She carryed the little boy in her arms.
f. I were late to school today.
   I was late to school today.

29. Fill the gaps with the past simple form of the verb in brackets.

On his first day in New Zealand he (get) _____ himself up early and (go) _____ to the kitchen for breakfast. He (is) _____ very nervous and not (eat) _____ much.

He (go) _____ to school in his homestay mother's car and (arrive) _____ at 8.30am.

All the new students (go) _____ to the office and the International Dean (meet) _____ them and (take) _____ them to the ESOL classroom. She (welcome) _____ the new students and (take) _____ them for a tour of the school.

30. Write the past tense form of the following irregular verbs.

Example: run   *ran*

a. go   _____
b. come   _____
c. write   _____
d. eat   _____
e. sit   _____
f. make   _____
g. break   _____
h. sleep   _____

31. Write questions for the following answers.

Example: *How long did he study French?*
         He studied French for one year.

a. _____?
   He came to school with his brother.

b. _____?
   He had cereal and toast for breakfast.

c. _____?
   She watched TV last night.

d. _____?
   She went home on her last holiday.

GRAMMAR

Past simple tense

The main use of the past simple tense is to talk about things which happened at a definite time in the past. These things are completed actions. It can also be used to talk about things that are unlikely to happen in the present or the future.

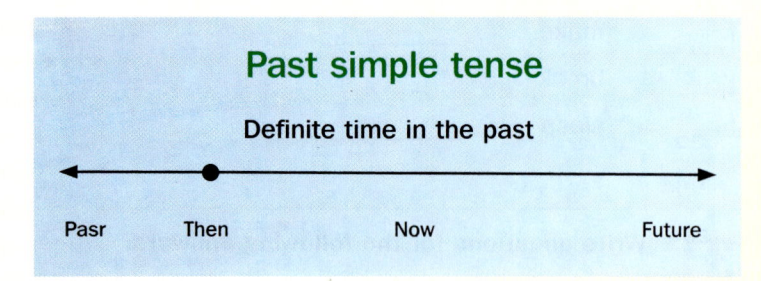

Past simple tense

Definite time in the past

Pasr — Then — Now — Future

Form

For regular verbs add *ed*. For example: *cook/cooked, talk/talked, hurry/hurried, carry/carried*.

Many verbs have irregular past tense forms. See the list at the end of the unit.

Questions in the past simple start with *did, was, were*. For example: *Did he go to school? Was your teacher late to school?*

Negatives in the past simple tense use *didn't, wasn't* and *weren't*. For example: *He didn't eat any breakfast. I wasn't late for school.*

VOCABULARY

attend / co-educational / Martian / planet / millennium / spectacular / tour / paper bag / flower / sugar / weigh / scales / deliver / strap / camera / vacuum cleaner / washing machine / disaster / suburb / cart(n)

TAPESCRIPTS

Tapescript 1

a. looked
b. worked
c. carried
d. talked
e. started
f. finished
g. travelled
h. asked
i. helped
j. copied

Tapescript 2

Back from Mars
by Kenn Nesbitt (from 'The Aliens Have Landed!')

I've recently returned from Mars.
I went for several years.
I rode in Martian motorcars,
bought Martian souvenirs.

I went to Martian movies
and saw Martian movie stars,
attended Martian concerts
and heard Martians play guitars.

I ate in Martian restaurants
and went to Martian schools.
I played on Martian tennis courts
and swam in Martian pools.

I hung around with Martian girls
and talked to Martian boys.
I went to Martian shopping malls
and played with Martian toys.

At last I'm back on planet Earth
from out among the stars.
So why does everyone I see here
act like they're from Mars?

Tapescript 3

I remember the night of the thirty-first of December 1999. It rained almost everywhere in New Zealand. But people all over the country stayed up to welcome in the new millennium. Gisborne is the first place to see the sun, so there was an official, traditional Maori ceremony on the beach despite the cold, wet conditions. I watched it on TV at home, but we could hear and see the fireworks that were being let off by braver people. Later in the day, we watched all the other countries in the world celebrate the New Year in many spectacular ways.

Common Irregular Verbs

Basic form	Past tense	Past participle
be	was/were	been
become	became	become
begin	began	begun
bite	bit	bitten
bleed	bled	bled
blow	blew	blown
break	broke	broken
bring	brought	brought
build	built	built
buy	bought	bought
catch	caught	caught
choose	chose	chosen
come	came	come
cut	cut	cut
do	did	done
drink	drank	drunk
drive	drove	driven
eat	ate	eaten
fall	fell	fallen
fight	fought	fought
find	found	found
fly	flew	flown
forget	forgot	forgotten
get	got	got
give	gave	given
go	went	gone
grow	grew	grown
have	had	had
hear	heard	heard
hit	hit	hit
hold	held	held
keep	kept	kept
know	knew	known
learn	learnt	learnt
make	made	made
put	put	put

Basic form	Past tense	Past participle
read	read	read
ride	rode	ridden
run	ran	run
say	said	said
send	sent	sent
shut	shut	shut
sit	sat	sat
sleep	slept	slept
speak	spoke	spoken
speed	sped	sped
stand	stood	stood
steal	stole	stolen
swim	swam	swum
teach	taught	taught
think	thought	thought
understand	understood	understood
wear	wore	worn
win	won	won
write	wrote	written

How Much Do You Remember?

Units 6–10

1. Write the comparative and superlative forms of the following adjectives.

Adjective	Comparative	Superlative
a. quick	_____	_____
b. big	_____	_____
c. friendly	_____	_____
d. kind	_____	_____
e. soft	_____	_____
f. tall	_____	_____
g. beautiful	_____	_____
h. expensive	_____	_____
i. unfriendly	_____	_____
j. handsome	_____	_____
k. good	_____	_____
l. bad	_____	_____

/6

2. Write down adjectives to describe the differences between the boy and the baby.

a. _____
b. _____
c. _____
d. _____
e. _____

/5

3. Write the correct form of the adjective in the gap.

a. Today is (hot) _____ than yesterday.
b. Today is the (hot) _____ day we have had this week.
c. He's the (short) _____ boy in the class.
d. She is the (helpful) _____ of the students.
e. She is a (good) _____ swimmer than her sister.
f. He won the (beautiful) _____ baby competition.
g. The actor who visited the school is (famous) _____ than the sportsman who came yesterday.
h. But Jonah Lomu is the (famous) _____ sportsman I know.

/4

4. Fill in the gaps with the present continuous form of the verb in brackets.

a. The boys (play) _____ rugby on the field.
b. The girls _____ (not play) soccer today.
c. I (go) _____ to the shops. Do you want to come?
d. They (study) _____ because they have exams next week.
e. We (go) _____ to the movies tonight.
f. It (rain) _____ so hard that we can hardly see the road.
g. We (get) _____ our hair done because we (go) _____ to the ball.
h. You must not go to sleep while the teacher (speak) _____ .
i. (Come) _____ you _____ to the party?

/5

How Much Do You Remember? Units 6-10

5. Write sentences that are true for you using the following words and the present continuous tense.

Example: *I wear socks. I am wearing socks. I am not wearing socks.*

a. I *do* maths. _____
b. It *rains*. _____
c. We *watch* a video. _____
d. They *go* home. _____

/4

6. Write the possessive forms of the following pronouns.

a. she _____
b. he _____
c. them _____
d. I _____
e. we _____
f. you _____

/3

7. Write a description of what this person is wearing.

8. Put the correct possessive pronoun in the gaps. (There may be more than one correct answer).

a. Is this _____ pen?
b. The boy said it was _____.
c. I am going to visit _____ grandparents.
d. Our dog is bigger than _____.
e. We are taking _____ dog for a walk.

/5

9. Write down what job each person does, and say what he/she is doing now.

a.  _____   b. _____

c.  _____   d. _____

e. _____

/4   /5

109

English Zone Elementary Student Book

10. Correct the following sentences.

a. A plumber mows lawns. _____
_____

b. A vet looks after sick children. _____
_____

c. A librarian works in a shop. _____
_____

d. I am doing my maths homework now. _____
_____

e. I am living in England. _____
_____

/5

11. Match the name of the job with what the person does by drawing a line between them.

a.	veterinarian	flies airplanes
b.	plumber	writes books
c.	author	looks after animals
d.	pilot	defends people in court
e.	lawyer	mends pipes and taps

/5

12. Put the correct form of the verb into the gaps (present simple or present continuous).

a. I (be) _____ a student and I (study) _____ English in New Zealand.

b. He (work) _____ in a restaurant but today he (have) _____ a day off.

c. I usually (ride) _____ my bike to school but today I (walk) _____ with you.

d. I (play) _____ hockey in winter, but now it is summer and I (play) _____ tennis.

e. He (drive) _____ an ambulance every day and right now he (hurry) _____ to an accident.

/5

13. Write two sentences about the occupation of the person and what each person is doing.

a. _____
_____

b. _____
_____

c. _____
_____

/6

14. Put *should*, *must*, *have to*, or *don't have to* into the gaps.

a. You _____ carry your licence with you if you are driving a car.

b. People _____ live in New Zealand for two years before sitting their licence.

c. You _____ insure your car.

d. Drivers _____ drive at 50 km per hour or less in built up area.

/4

15. Fill the gap with an infinitive of purpose.

a. He came to New Zealand _____ English.

b. I went to the post office _____ a letter.

c. She went to the shop _____ some food.

d. I opened my bag _____ my pen.

e. We went to the cinema _____ a movie.

/5

16. Write the past simple form of the following verbs.

a. carry _____
b. talk _____
c. go _____
d. run _____
e. travel _____
f. come _____
g. finish _____
h. have _____
i. make _____
j. eat _____

/5

17. Fill the gaps with *did*, *was* or *were*.

a. When _____ you leave your home country?

b. Why _____ you late to school today?

c. What _____ you have for breakfast?

d. What _____ the weather like yesterday?

e. When _____ you start at this school?

/5

18. Write the following sentences as negatives.

a. I ran to school this morning.
_____

b. She came to school by car.
_____

c. I was tired so I went to bed early.
_____

d. I saw that movie when I was at home.
_____

e. He lived with his mother until he was forty years old.
_____

/5

19. Write the words which match the definitions.

a. e_____ costs a lot of money

b. p_____ the number of people who live in a certain place

c. f_____ to be well known

d. b_____ a formal dance

e. t_____ a way of doing something which has existed for a long time

f. e_____ someone who takes what we have and turns it into what we need

g. p_____ a strong feeling

h. c_____ something you must do is …

i. i_____ the place where two or more roads meet

j. r_____ a vehicle that meets all the requirements for safety on the road

k. f_____ a style of clothes

l. l_____ an official document that gives you permission to do something

/6

111

English Zone Elementary Student Book

20. Write the meaning of each sign in the space provided.

a. _____

b. _____

c. _____

d. _____

e. _____

f. _____

g. _____

h. _____

i. _____

j. _____

/5

TOTAL   /100

112